TAPPING THE POWER WITHIN

A Path to Self-Empowerment for Black Women

IYANLA VANZANT

Harlem River Press
New York • London

Acknowledgment is given with love for use and
expansion of the teachings/writings of:

Lolita Rodriquez
Mary Cruz
Olúwo Osun Kunle
Chief Adenibi Äjamu, Ifa Muyiwa
Ade Ifaleri Olayinka
Osho
J. Omosade Awolalu
Kofi Asare Opoku
John S. Mbiti
Ron Norwood
Linda "Shaheerah" Beatty
Morning Star
Eva Bailey
Egun Ye
CARMEN

Published by **WRITERS AND READERS PUBLISHING, INCORPORATED** for

HARLEM RIVER PRESS
P.O. Box 461, Village Station
New York, N.Y. 10014

c/o Airlift Book Company
26 Eden Grove
London N7 8EF
England

Text copywright © 1992 Iyanla Vanzant.
Cover design: Terrie Dunkelberger.

Library of Congress Catalog Card Number: 92-072216
ISBN: 0-86316-140-5 (trade)
    4 5 6 7 8 9 0
Manufactured in the United States of America

For My Mothers

Sarah Jefferson, Nancy McCullum
Lynnette Harris, Yemoja and Oshun

and My Daughters

Gemmia, Nisa, Dr. Duro Jaiye Onisegun, Ebun, Lucille,
Sheshimi, Irene, Nzinga, Marcie, Zuri and Tania

Iyanla Vanzant, born in Brooklyn, New York, is a Yoruba
Priestess, lawyer and empowerment specialist. Cofounder of
Inner Visions Spiritual Life Maintenance Network, she lives in the
Washington D.C. area with her daughters and grandchildren.

When you come to the end of all the light
that you know,

And, you are about to step off into
darkness,

FAITH

is knowing one of two things will happen:

There will be something solid in the darkness
for you to stand on . . .

OR,

You will be taught how to fly!

HAVE FAITH

Dr. Jordan
Margaret Paul

CONTENTS

READINGS FOR
FURTHER STUDY

Afrika, Llaila: African Holistic Health

Bradshaw, John: Healing The Shame That Binds You
The Family
Home Coming: Healing the Inner Child

Black Elk, Wallace: Black Elk Speaks: Wisdom of the Lakota

Foundation For
Inner Peace: A Course In Miracles

Gurudas: The Spiritual Properties of Herbs

Hollies, Linda: Inner Healing For Broken Vessels

Idowu, Bolaji: Olodumare: God In Yoruba Belief

Karenga, Maulana: The Husia: Sacred Teachings of
Ancient Egypt

Kinnear, Willis: 30-Day Mental Diet

Mason, John: Black Gods: Orisa Concepts In the
New World

Mbiti, John S.:   Introduction to African Religion
African Religion and Philosophy

Roman Sanaya: Spiritual Growth: Being Your
Higher Self

White Eagle: Spiritual Unfoldment 1,2,3,4

Whittaker, Terry Cole: What You Think of Me Is None
of My Business

INTRODUCTION

This book is offered to assist you on your journey toward peace, success and freedom—to be who you are. It is the first step in your journey back to the beginning— your journey in "spirit." Written from the perspective of the ancient Yoruba culture and universal knowledge, the information presented is based on the premise that you are a divine expression of the Creator, Olodumare (which means God in Yoruba language). As you pass from the world of spirit (the womb) into the physical world, Olodumare (God) gave you the gift of life. That gift is "breath."

You are, in essence, spirit, housed in a physical envelope, brought to life by the breath of God to fulfill a divine mission. Your mission, while different from that of all other living beings, is directed toward a common goal—harmonious interaction among all living creatures and service for the good of the universe. As spirit, you know your destiny. You were informed prior to your birth. You choose, as spirit, the time, place, location and circumstances of your physical life. As spirit, you are fully aware of what you must do, learn and overcome in order to fulfill your mission. In the physical form, you were given hands, feet, intelligence and the discretion to fend for yourself. To be able to clearly understand and accomplish your mission, it is necessary to coordinate the spiritual and the physical self.

How do you achieve spiritual/physical coordination? How do you find the correct path for your spiritual mission? How do you fulfill your divine destiny? You do this with your breath and your thoughts. It is by breath and with breath that you can direct the course of your life. Sounds simple right? Well believe it or not, life is simple. Life is the simple in-and-out flow of events, circumstances and people. We make it difficult by cutting off, holding on and trying to control the flow. All we ever need to do is be conscious. We must breath consciously and live consciously. We must learn to let things flow just like breath and life will do the rest.

Your spirit will guide you through the flow of life. As your link to the Creator, spirit is all-knowing, all-powerful and ever-present. Spirit is divine, and so are you. It is sometimes difficult to accept that people are so divine. It is particularly difficult for African Americans who have been oppressed, disenfranchised, miseducated, culturally and spiritually raped. The key is to "believe" you are divine; to "accept" that you have spiritual rights and to "know" that your ancestors, the universe and the Creator are supporting you spiritually.

You should understand that as an African descendant, spirit and spirituality are a wholesome element of your basic nature. You are not replacing or undermining God in developing your spirit, you are trying to make contact with the powerful force that is God within you. What you are seeking and searching for has always been with you. You have now consciously decided to explore, accept and understand how to make it work for you and with you.

The principle element of your spiritual growth and physical evolution is the understanding of your self and your experiences. Nothing in this world is new. It has all been done and said before. Africans, as the parent race, have established the principles for understanding and confronting life issues. The principles are what we call tradition and culture. It is through these mediums that our ancestors developed a standard of behavior, and a code of morality, ethics and values which should govern thoughts and actions for the fullest expression of life. Our ancestors determined five principles which, if applied to daily life activities, will reap positive spiritual and physical results. They are: 1) Truth; 2) Order; 3) Justice; 4) Faith; and, 5) Patience. These principles, when followed and utilized as the foundations of our actions, decisions and interactions will put us in touch with the highest universal forces. When we act in contradiction to these principles, our lives become chaotic, disorderly, and stagnant. In our pain, misery and confusion, we lay blame and seek solutions outside of ourselves. The key is to "begin within."

Anything and everything you have experienced has been purposeful—it has brought you to where you are now. If you are fat and happy, thin and sad, wealthy and miserable, poor and sick, you have a collection of experiences to use as steppingstones to take you where you want to go. Like cotton which grows in an ugly thorny pad and is transformed into beautiful color garments, you can transform your experiences into beautiful lessons. How?

By changing the way you think about them.

As you embark upon this journey, be gentle with yourself. Do not think this is a "quick fix" to the challenges you face and do not set unrealistic goals for obtaining spiritual insights. "You must eat the mountain one bite at a time." You must be willing to release worn-out thoughts, habits and situations in order to receive and put to use the information spirit will bring you. Be patient and above all, be open to receive and grow. Do not be afraid to look at your faults, for when you recognize them, you have the power to change them.

When you begin your quest for spiritual growth, keep your own counsel. Do not try to convince others that what you are doing is right for you or for them. Everyone will get what they need, when they need it. As you grow and develop, everything and everyone in your environment will respond accordingly. Very often, things and people will fall away from you. Do not hold on. Know that you cannot lose anything or anyone within the "divine" order of your life. You can pray for your beloved ones and others without seeking their approval of your spiritual growth. Remember, you cannot want more for others than they want for themselves. Your first responsibility is to you. Be good to yourself, be honest with yourself and others. Understanding that we all, in our own way, are pefect expressions of the Creator's life force.

The energy of Olodumare is with you through spirit. Your mission is to tap into it. The Time Is Now!

Towards Enlightenment,

Iyanla.

FOREWORD

Each of us has the innate, God-given ability to know all there is to know. This ability can manifest at any given time as a personal quality and information which enables one to achieve peace, success, prosperity and well being. This ability is known as the "power" of spirit. For African Americans in particular, this understanding is vitually important. Throughout a history of oppression, cultural disenfranchisement and miseducation, African Americans have relinquished their spiritual power to those who appeared to be more powerful than themselves. The power is readily available to all who are willing to give of themselves and claim it.

The empowerment process is accomplished by unity of the will with the unlimited power source of "spirit." The will is the master male principle. The conscious ability to think, to choose, to do. The spirit is the master female principle. The moving, creative, life-nurturing force in the universe. These two principles, although often unrecognized, are present throughout the universe in many forms: Yin and Yang energy; the conscious (male) and unconscious (female) mind; the sperm and egg. Each of these is a symbolic representation of the masculine and feminine energies. Spiritual insights begins when one understands the purpose of unity between these complementary forces. One can then use these innate energies to fulfill their divine mission.

We can exercise the will at any given time, much in the same way as a male produces sperm continuously. However, the union of the will and spirit, must take place under the same conditions which allow the sperm to penetrate the egg at the right time. If one is in tune with universal timing and purpose, one can impregnate the spirit with the energy of the will to create their own fate. Will and spirit are connected by the "breath." When you are in control of your breathing, you are the facilitator of a divine union. Armed with this knowledge, artificial barriers such as racism, sexism, poverty and fear can be dismantled. Any individual moving on spiritual power, cannot be limited.

Unity of the will and spirit has been impeded by man's unconscious exercise of will to satisfy physical, emotional and sexual desires, and unconscious breathing. Old tapes from childhood, the education process, and enculturation create patterns and practices toward which we direct our will. We recognize the unproductive thoughts, words and deeds which contribute to our physical and spiritual dissatisfaction. Yet, we are seemingly unable to make necessary modifications of our attitudes and behaviors. Dysfunctional belief systems inherited from family, community and societal influences further complicate our ability to unite the will and spirit. Traditional African societies created and practiced spiritual techniques which enabled the individual to direct thought, will and action in a constructive manner. These practices facilitate an internal spiritual empowerment which brings the individual into alignment with universal energy.

In an ancient story of the sower, we meet a farmer who casts his seeds willfully, without purpose. Some seeds fell upon hard and rocky ground. Unable to root, they did not produce. Others fell on fertile ground and produced a bounty of crops. Still others, undirected, fell in heaps and were eaten by birds. The seeds represent what occurs to our thoughts when we act without unity of will and spirit. This story demonstrates how we are conditioned to approach life. We are vaguely in touch with our purpose and function. We know there are things we must do. However, we often approach life in a automatic mode. We concentrate on the physical stimuli, based on titles, structure and imposed expectations. Many are unaware of the need to unite the physical with the spiritual.

The hard rocky ground represents a state of awareness influenced by external factors. It is referred to as "Dharana." This is a state of survival where one is focused on the physical environment. Since the physical world represents only one-tenth of objective reality, it is impossible to view life accurately from this state. It is impossible to produce seeds of positive thought and action from this state. The heaped seeds represent thoughts which are undirected, unfocused and are counteracted by the ingrained conditioning expressed by our habitual thoughts and behaviors. It is referred to as "Dhyana," w   we move automatically on a physical level, our tho undirected and out of touch with our actions. thrown in fertile ground represent the union of th spirit. Referred to as "Samadhi," it is in this thoughts and actions are charged by the life force to produce a bountiful harvest. The life force which charges the union of will and spirit is what we call emotions, "the energy that moves."

Imagine that you are walking down the street. You are aware of everything around you. You notice the houses, the trees, the cars and people. You are in a state of survival, aware of the physical level, the body. You are in Dharana. You continue walking, eventually looking up to realize you have walked five blocks. You remember walking only two blocks. Unaware, you slipped into the state of Dhyana, where your physical actions become automatic. Your thoughts were elsewhere. You arrive at the corner and stop. Your mind drifts to the vision of yourself holding your child. You can hear, smell and feel the essence of the child. You are no longer aware of your surroundings. The sound of a honking horn brings you back to the physical consciousness. You have experienced a state of "Samadhi," unaware of the physical, totally at-oneness with the thought. The "in-sperience" of the thoughts of your child created an emotional bonding of your will. The will, unhindered by the physical world, impregnated your spirit to create a reality. It is this ability of the individual to connect with the essence of their being that enables them to control their fate. This connection and realization is the result of the conscious effort to unite the will and the spirit.

The book you are about to read will assist you in creating a unity of will and spirit. It should not be approached like a novel. It will provide you with guidance for moving from the survival state to the consciousness of aligning the mind (will) and spirit. In these pages, you will find breathing and meditative techniques which, when diligently applied, will empower you to move to a state of alignment and enlightenment. This alignment is sure to produce a positive impact on your life. It manifests as your ability to unite with your deepest desires for the good of yourself, your family and the world, unhindered by physical encumbrances. Ancient African philosophy teaches us that we need not know how to move obstacles. We need only the courage, knowledge and wisdom which will take us around them. With this in mind, we invite you to "Tap The Power Within" yourself; the source of your goodness, your greatness, your birthright. "Let all who have ears hear" these words and move toward the power.

Saluting Your Greatness,

Sekhter Uanuf,

Vice President, rookKing, Inc.

* *Dharana, Dhyana and Samadhi are words taken from the Vedantic tradition.*

CHAPTER 1

Spirit

Growing up as a dark-skinned child, with short hair, a broad nose and thin legs, it was difficult for me to find anything beautiful about myself. My brother didn't help matters any. He told me that I had graduated from ugly to oogly, which was a cross between a mistake and a disaster. It became a family joke. He told me, " . . . when God said beauty, you thought he said doodie, and ran off to the bathroom." That's how he explained my lack of good looks. I was convinced I was ugly and I "knew" everyone else thought I was ugly too.

As a young girl I spent many hours peering in the mirror, praying for beauty. My mother's lipstick, barrettes and hairbows from Woolworth's or Lady Ester's Cold

Cream offered little help. If I were going to find beauty, I would have to look some place other than the mirror which reflected my face. One day, a strange thing happened. I was about 12 at the time. I was sitting at my normal spot on the bathroom sink with one foot propped on the toilet for balance. I was staring at myself in the mirror when I saw a burst of colors behind me. I froze. My heart was racing. I was looking at a reflection of myself I had never seen before. I was tall, dressed in a long flowing white robe. My hair, eyes and mouth were the same, yet there was a glow around my face. I was beautiful.

The reflection in the mirror reached out to me. I panicked and my foot slipped into the toilet. The reflection smiled. I heard someone say, "Take my hand. Come closer." My mind was a blur, but I remember repositioning myself and peering deeper into the mirror. The reflection of me now had a bright blue glow. I heard the voice again, "All your beauty is within. It is your power. All you need do is look within." The reflection faded; as I was jolted back to the moment, I fell off the sink. On the way down, I hit my head on the tub and my mouth on the tile floor. Somebody knocked. "You ok in there?" "Yeah, I must have fallen asleep." I scrambled to my feet and glared at myself in the mirror. I had a huge bump on my head. My bottom lip was swollen and bleeding. I looked an awful mess. I stared at my reflection as tears welled up in my eyes. I wanted that beautiful reflection of me to re-appear. It didn't. So now, not only was I oogly, I was bruised. What's a girl to do?

Spirit is the life force of every living element. It is the life essence which is covered and protected by the skeletal frame or flesh we call the body. Spirit is the energy of the Creator coming forth in many forms. Within the human being, spirit is the divine, noble, immortal essence which cannot be destroyed and never dies. Spirit lives by virtue of blood and breath which continues to flow through the birth of another of the same kind. Spirit has no color. Spirit has no gender. Spirit has only one purpose and mission which is determined by God at the time of creation.—Everything that has life, can create life, nurtures life or serves a purpose in life, is spirit. The Creator's goal is for every spirit to learn to serve one another and live in peace-filled harmony. Spirit, therefore, lives on many levels. Those we can see and those we cannot see. A living being is a form of spirit we can see. One who has lived and no longer breathes, is a form of spirit we can no longer see. African culture teaches that spirit also exists in many forms, some of which we do not recognize. This concept helps us to understand that minerals, plants and animals are also considered spirit. Fire is another example of a living form we do not recognize as spirit. In its life, the energy of fire can be constructive, as in a cooking flame, or destructive, as in the burning of a home. As human beings, our primary goal should be to seek a life which will allow our spirit to be a constructive force.

In Yoruba culture the essence of the human being is called "Emi." Emi is the link between man and God, which is sustained by breathing. Emi, or soul, is that part of man which returns to God at the end of the physical existence. Emi is the pure, impersonal, divine energy that exists in everyone. What governs and guides Emi is the sacred energy called "Ori," the spiritual and physical inner head. To the Yoruba, Ori represents the unity of the spiritual and physical being. Ori is that part of man which maintains the knowledge of the individual's spiritual and physical life mission. Ori knows what we must accomplish and learn during our life time. Ori is developed through experiences. It manifests as our personality. It takes on the characteristics of our gender. It governs our ability and the motivations by which we make choices and decisions. Our primary mission in life should be to keep our "Emi" (soul) and "Ori" (spirit) in alignment. This alignment is called "ache"—power or truth. It is only by following the promptings and guidance of your own ache that you can successfully fulfill your spiritual and physical life mission according to the will of the Creator.

Spirit is the essence which gives meaning to life. For this purpose, life is defined as, "Learning Inspired For Evolution." The evolution of life is the process of preparation, refinement and improvement for a greater purpose. Our physical life is the learning process in which we are spiritually purified. The purification takes place when we learn as a result of our experiences in life. Learning is a spiritual process by which we are refined and prepared to be of greater service to other living beings. However, in order to be physically and spiritually purified, we must bring our Ori (spirit) and physical mind into alignment with the laws of nature.—The Creator has established the natural laws which facilitate the purification and learning process we call life. These laws are what we call seasons, causes, effects, balance, harmony, righteousness and order. Our Ori (spirit) knows, in intricate detail, which of the laws we must learn and align with during our lifetime. Ori then guides us to the experiences we will need in order to learn. Ori, then, serves as the recorder of the choices and decisions we make which are and are not in alignment with natural law. When we are in contact with our Ori and follow its guidance, what we know as our first thought, we are continuously provided with opportunities to bring ourselves into alignment with natural law. When we are in alignment we can recognize and accept the lessons which will lead us to a fuller, more peace-filled and purposeful sense of living.—Our greatest challenge in the learning, purification and alignment process of life is our mind. The mind, expressing our will and ego, is developed as a result of our experiences, emotions and intelligence. But mind, ego and will are not in alignment with natural or spiritual laws. They are concerned with the way things "appear" to be, not what our experiences teach us on the spiritual level. It is only with a conscious effort that we can infuse the will and ego with the energy and power of the spirit.—When the will and ego are not in alignment with our spiritual mind (Ori) we have what the Yoruba's call, "a bad head." It is what grandmother's in this country call being "hardheaded." This means that we live for physical pleasures and pursuits without conscious contact with the true essence of our being. When we have a bad head, we rely on the ego to determine what we need. The needs we perceive we have lead us to actions which usually create negative experiences. These needs are also created by emotions which result from our negative experiences. Our mind will mesh together what we experience and desire to form a thought. Although thoughts govern how we respond throughout life, they may not be in alignment with the spiritual purpose or meaning of the experience. When we respond to physical thought alone, we are distracted by opinions, fears, the limitations of our experiences and the influences of others. It is on this level of thinking that we encounter the challenges and obstacles we often refer to as the problems of life.

African Americans, torn away from our ancestral cultures, have lost touch with the process of connecting with our spirit self. We are no longer socialized or encouraged to pursue a spiritual life style. We have been taught/told who we are, what we need; why we need it and how to go about getting what we have been told we need. Our perceptions have been molded in a hostile environment. Our egos have been attuned to the physical world in pursuit of social and material gain. We rarely trust or follow our natural instincts. We seek validation in books while pursuing credentials in hope that we will be accepted by others who are also out of alignment. In this process, our Ori (spirit), which is endowed with the knowledge of our unique life lessons and spiritual mission lies dormant. "Spirit will never push or ask to come forward. It will wait to be invited." If we are to realize the true essence of our being and meaning in life, we must turn within to find the guidance of spirit and bring ourselves, individually and collectively, into alignment with spirit.—What I had seen in the mirror when I was 12, was my spirit. My true identity. The intensity of my thought, fused with the emotional desire to be beautiful, drew the essence of my being to the physical level. Spirit was clothed in a form I could recognize. It spoke in a manner I could comprehend. My spirit let me know on that day many years ago, what we seek without, we must first find within. I wanted physical beauty. What I failed to realize is the physical body has no power or meaning of its own. The body exists only as an extension of spirit. What we think and feel will create our reality because spirit creates from the inside to the outside. We must therefore see it within first.—"Tapping the Power Within" is a process of recognition and reliance on the spirit that exists within us all. Spirit is the presence and the power of the Creator which is sustained by breath. It is that spirit within which will provide us with the power to control our lives. Control from a spiritual perspective means "knowing." When you know what to do, how to do it and why you are doing it, you are in control. Knowing brings you into alignment with the law. You are learning lessons. You are creating divine order in your life. You are fulfilling your unique mission. You are experiencing the purification which will prepare your spirit on its path of evolution.

Beyond the spirit of self are various levels of energy which can be instrumental in spiritual growth. African culture teaches that we must recognize spirit on all levels. Spirits of air, water, fire and earth are called "nature spirits." They provide us with the essential elements that support our physical life. Animal spirits represent the basic instinct of all living creatures to survive and thrive on the earth's provisions. Ancestral spirits represent the energy of those who have departed the physical plane and now exist on another level of energy. They represent the energy of life purifying itself. Ancestral spirits are represented by the standards, structures, values and institutions which are an integral part of life as we know it. Ancestors may be of the family, community, race or nation. According to Yoruba culture, ancestral spirits are called "Egungun."

ANCESTRAL SPIRITS

To avoid confusion regarding ancestral spirits, this brief explanation is offered. The principle foundation of African spiritual philosophy and culture is the concept that life is a continuous process. Spirit, as the link to life and the Creator, takes on various forms, at various times, in order to fulfill a mission. Spirit may move from the visible to the invisible level as part of the evolutionary process. In its visible physical form, spirit is the person. In its invisible form, spirit is energy. Ancestral spirits are those persons in the family, community, race or nation, who no longer house a physical form, yet their energy is still among us as a result of their living.

Ancestor worship is an integral element of African spiritual culture. It is the method of honoring those who have laid the foundation in this life. It is important that African Americans have a clear understanding before they accept or reject the practice. In calling the name, giving praise or honoring an ancestor, you are not worshipping the person. Remember—spirit is energy. It is not a personality. When spirit leaves the physical body, it is no longer hindered by character flaws, personality disorders or the emotional imbalances which may have been present during the individual's lifetime. The individual spirit has attained a new level of enlightenment as a result of life experiences. The prayers and mental energy offered to the spirit of an ancestor serves to lift the energy of the spirit toward the process of evolution. It is perfectly acceptable to call upon an ancestor you did not know or one you did not have favorable relations with in your life. Your lesson is forgiveness and acceptance. The lesson of the spirit is alignment and purification. Just as people in your life have helped you to learn and evolve, your prayers will do the same for the spirit.

Family ancestors are sustained by virtue of your life. Their blood runs through your veins. They are a vital link in your chain of existence, since without any one of them, you would not be who you are. Your living means they have contact with the physical and spiritual planes. Community, racial and national ancestors are those, who through their work and contributions while on the physical plane, benefitted the community, race or nation. Harriet Tubman, W.E.B. Dubois, Frederick Douglass, El Hajj Malik Shabazz, Soujourner Truth (to name a few), are racial and national ancestors. We pay homage to them

through the furtherance of their work and the maintenance of the institutions they built. The maintenance of
a property or land which had significance to an ancestor
is one of the highest forms of honor and worship.

According to African philosophy, recognition of
ancestral spirits is vital to spiritual growth and evolution.
These spirits exist as energy in our environment and are
most concerned about our day-to-day survival. Think
back to what your grandmother, aunt, mother, father or
anyone of your family ancestors did for you during their
life. Even if the relations between you were strained, seek
to recognize the energy contribution they made to your
life. In the spiritual form, the energy of these ancestors has
changed. The spirit, freed from the physical body, has a
duty to assist you. This assistance may come in the form
of a dream, an inspiration, or an opportunity. It is spirit
helping spirit to fulfill the Creator's work. Your job, on the
physical level, is to keep that energy alive through recognition, honor and veneration. The simplest form of honoring ancestral spirits is by calling their name. You can do
this formally, through prayer, or informally. You may
want to set up an ancestral altar or shrine. You may simply
thank them for protection and guidance. Remember, you
are not dealing with a person, you are incorporating
energy.

PRAYER FOR ANCESTRAL SPIRITS

*I give praise and thanksgiving to the omnipotent
    Creator.*

*I give praise to the light and energy of the four
    directions.*

*I give praise to the light and energy of the air I breathe,
I offer you food so that your spirits may grow stronger, and
more powerful.*

*I offer you flowers, a gift of the earth so that you will know
there are descendants who remember and respect your
presence.*

*I ask you Spirit Mothers, Fathers, Brothers, Sisters and friends
to remember me in your travels.*

*Protect me. Guide me. Assist me and all members of our
family, living and dead.*

*I am in need of your assistance at all times to overcome
challenges and obstacles with money, health, employment
and my own mortal progress.*

*I thank you for your guidance. I thank you for your
intercession in the matter of_____(here you would
state the area in which you need assistance.)*

*Good spirits, carry my prayers with you to the feet of the
Creator.*

Still my heart and mind with perfect peace and resolve.

*I thank you for bringing the perfect solution, in the
perfect way, at the perfect time, for the best of all involved.*

So Be It.

GUARDIAN SPIRITS

Every living being has a God-appointed guardian spirit which walks through life with you. This good spirit unites with you at the moment you are born. Some refer to it as, "guardian angel" or "protector spirit." In African culture, guardian spirits are called, "Egun." It is the duty of your Egun to assist you on your life path. Like the spirit of your head (Ori), the Egun waits for acknowledgment and recognition. It will not interfere with the choices or decisions of your conscious mind. However, in times of need or danger, this spirit will give guidance and insight in the form of thoughts or presentiments. When you follow the direction given by your Egun, also called "your first thought," you can overcome many challenges and obstacles.

A guardian spirit may be an ancestral spirit or some other benevolent force whose spiritual evolution is dedicated to assisting living beings. While ancestral spirits have a vested interest in the survival of their descendants, they are not always guardians for their living family line. A guardian spirit may be an acquaintance from a previous life existence or a highly evolved soul who is appointed to assist in your care. Unlike your Ori, the guardian exists outside of your physical body. However, it is within your "spiritual reach" at all times.

Guardian spirits may or may not have names. You may call it "my guardian," Egun," "my protector," or any common name you choose. In a state of relaxation and meditation, you can ask the spirit for its name. The response will be in the form of a thought. You may have a dream in which you see a person who is familiar but you cannot remember their name. Chances are it was your guardian spirit. Males may have female guardians; females may have male guardians, they are appointed based upon their past life experiences and your present life mission. Consequently, your Egun, or guardian spirit, is most probably of the same race and ethnic background as you are.

In addition to your principal guardian spirit, there are other benevolent spirits who assist you in life. Those of the Catholic faith refer to them as Saints. Others may acknowledge universal spirits or earth spirits. These highly evolved, sympathetic forces unite with your guardian at various times to assist you in confronting your challenges. You may experience it as a burst of energy, or an onslaught of information or opportunities. The key is to become focused and centered, and ask your Egun for clarity and guidance.

To contact or communicate with your guardian spirit, you must simply be open and willing to do so. Your guardian spirit remains with you whether or not you recognize its presence. However, recognition, praise and thanksgiving of your guardian spirit will strengthen its presence and influence in your life. Guardian spirits are ministers and messengers of the Creator. They provide another valuable link to universal intelligence and divine power. They walk with you, stand beside you and care for you throughout life.

Prayer is the best method of communication with your Eguns. You may want to erect an altar for your guardian spirit to assist you in maintaining constant contact and recognition. To set up an altar you need:

1. A small table covered with white cloth.
2. A large vessel of water (to purify the channels of spiritual communication).
3. White flowers (nature's gift of beauty, birth and love).

4. A white candle (to foster energy and communication).

This basic set-up brings the four power elements of the universe together—air, water, fire and earth—and provides a source of concentrated energy. (For a more elaborate altar see "Water".)

The key to any spiritual process is your mind. You must be willing to surrender your ego to a higher spiritual force. As a living being, you are linked to the power of all spirits. Through your Ori, you have the keys and secrets to your unique mission. Your challenge is to surrender what you think to what you are intuitively told to do. This is not an easy task. You must overcome years of conditioning, the influences of your environment and the desire to be in control. You cannot receive spiritual consciousness with reasoning or intelligence. Focus. Trust. Have unquestioning faith.—Recognizing ancestral spirits, guardian spirits and the spirit of your head is the foundation of spiritual evolution according to African culture. For African American women, it is a process by which we can overcome all physical limitations and live a life of service and healing. It does not matter what religious path a woman chooses. What will determine destiny is the degree to which we strive to bring forth the essence of spirit. At the spiritual level, a woman is the divine expression of love. She is co-creator with God, capable of bringing forth new life. A spiritual woman is a healer, teacher, and nurturer of life, because it is her ability to love that will soothe all who come into contact with her.—The following is an ageless prayer dedicated to universal guardian spirits. Daily repetitions will provide spiritual strength and guidance.

PRAYER FOR GUARDIAN SPIRITS

Prudent and benevolent spirits,
Messenger of God (the Creator, Divine Spirit).
Your mission is to assist me and guide me by
      by the good path.
I thank you for your support.
Help me to endure the tests of this life and
      accept them without complaint.
Deviate from me all negative thoughts.
Please do not let me give access to dark spirits
      who intend to make me fail in the progress
      of love for myself and all fellow beings.
Take from my eyes the veil of pride which prevents
      me from seeing my own defects and from
      confessing them to myself.
Above all my guardian spirit, I know you are
      the one who protects me and takes an
      interest in me.
You know my necessities. Please guide me
      and assist me in accordance to the will
      and in the grace of the Creator.
I welcome your presence, your guidance and
      your assistance.
Thank you pure spirit.*

*Adapted from, <u>Collection of Selected Prayers</u> by Alan Dardec. For additional reading see Ibid. and the <u>The Spirits Book</u> also by Kardec.

GUARDIAN SPIRIT ALTAR

Chapter 2

Spirituality

I was sleeping, minding my own business when the first chill went through my body. The scenes began to play out in vivid color. My son Damon was sitting on the floor in a dark room. He wasn't tied up but I sensed that he couldn't move. I was standing in the room. I called out to him. He seemed not to hear me. I could hear the voices of several men. I knew they were angry and dangerous. I felt the panic flood my mind and body. I ran out of the room calling for Damon to follow me. He didn't move.

I was running down a long hallway screaming my son's name. I looked back over my shoulder to see that the men had entered the room. I stopped running. I turned back to face the room. I saw one of the men hit Damon. My heart sank. I started walking back toward the room. I was crying. "Please stop." "Please don't." One of the men had a gun. I started running back toward the room. I heard the gun click. I came to a dead halt. The gun clicked again. I screamed. The telephone rang. I sat up in the bed. I was sweating and panting. The telephone rang again. It was 6:03 a.m. Saturday morning.

I grabbed for the telephone, knocking it to the floor. My chest was heaving so hard I couldn't speak. I put the phone to my ear. "Ma?" It was my oldest daughter calling me from Morgan State University where she was a freshman student. "Why are you calling me at this time of the morning?" It sounded frightening to hear my own voice. "Ma, you've got to find Damon." Then she told me about her dream. She and her brother were running from a mob of people. She didn't know why the people were chasing them. Damon kept falling down. She would stop to help him up, and they would run a little farther. Finally the mob caught up with them. They encircled them. Damon was arguing with the people, but she kept pulling him to run away. When they did start running again, they were able to put a great distance between themselves and the mob. Finally they stopped running to rest. She remembered that she was fine but Damon was sweating and panting. He was bent over trying to catch his breath. She was looking right at him when a huge black truck came from nowhere and hit her brother.

I told my daughter to pack her clothes. I called a friend of mine and told her I needed to rent a car. She never asked why. She told me to make the arrangements and let her know what time we could pick the car up. I had $40 in cash, but somehow I knew I would make it from Philadelphia to Maryland, and from Maryland to Norfolk, Virginia.

My son had recently been discharged from the Navy. He, his wife, and their baby were living somewhere in Norfolk. They did not have a telephone. I had an address and no idea of where I was going. I picked up the car about

1 p.m. When I dropped her off, my friend put $50 in my hand. I pulled up to my daughter's dorm at Morgan at about 2:30 p.m. It was 9 p.m. when I turned the car off the highway on to Oceanview Road in Norfolk. I told my daughter that the area looked vaguely familiar. I told her to check the parking lots we passed for my son's car. We had driven about 10 miles when I pulled into a motel parking lot where we had seen several cars with New York license plates. As I turned into the lot and prepared to park, my son Damon ran across the lot on his way to the telephone.

My son was living in a motel on the busiest thorough-fare in Norfolk, selling drugs. He and another young man about 18 years old had started their "business" with their tax return money. He estimated that they were making between $5,000 and $7,500 a day. A rival dealer had put a hit out on them. That morning, two of the gunmen cornered my son in the motel. They informed him that they really wanted the other guy and that when they found him, and if my son was with him, he, too, would pay the consequences. He said that it had happened about 5 a.m. that morning. Over the course of the next two days, I took the 18 year old home to his mother, sent his 16-year-old girlfriend home to her mother, dropped two pearl-handled pistols in the ocean and packed my son up and moved him back to New York. I thank God every day that He gave me the opportunity to help save my son. Since that day, when the spirit says jump, I ask "How High?"

Spirituality means of the spirit. It is a oneness within and without. Within there is a sense of peace, balance and knowing that you are an integral part of a dynamic whole. That whole is life, expressing itself in many ways and supporting the evolution of all life's expressions.

Without, spirituality is a connection to every living force in nature and the universe. This connection provides unlimited resources and a sense of being complete. Spirituality is reliance on your internal universe as the vehicle to carry you through the journey of life. It is a universal connection to everyone and everything. The connection of spirituality means accepting that you are not your brother's keeper. It means knowing that you are your brother by the oneness of spirit.

To live a life guided by spirit is to live a life of spirituality. It is the result of aligning the physical mind with the spiritual mind. Spirituality requires relaxation of the conscious mind, suppression of the ego, and reliance on divine universal energy as the motivating life force. When one relies on spirit, the divine essence of the being—the physical life—becomes an expression of well-being.

Spirituality means faith in self as a divine and noble expression of the Creator and faith in spirit as your guide in life. Spirituality means viewing life through a spirit's eye—the third eye which is not limited by ego, perception or intelligence. Spirituality means seeing the truth, value and beauty in all life forces and dedicating one's self to the expansion of those lives. Spirituality is a journey inward which connects you to the pulse of the universe as it is expressed through your being.

When you know who you are from the inside out; when you do what you sense is right for you regardless of what others are saying or doing; when your first point of reference is your own thought; and, when your thoughts lead you to actions which serve others as well as make you feel good, you have encountered spirituality. Spirituality, the alignment of the physical and spiritual minds, creates "a good head." A good head utilizes the divine spark of spirit as the motivating force of thought, words and actions. Spirituality is recognition of your connection to the essence of the Creator as the source of your power. Spirituality is not religion, for it does not matter to which church you belong or the religious philosophy you follow. Religion is the way, the rules and regulations used to approach the concept of God. Spirituality simply means that you recognize and accept your individual connection to the Creator and use that "spiritual connection" as your guiding force. This connection brings you peace, fulfillment, happiness and abundance because it enables you to overcome the limitations of the physical mind and body by putting you in touch with the true source of power — the spirit of the Creator.

Spirituality conquers fear, hate, anger, loneliness and deprivation. It replaces these ideas with purpose, love, worthiness, understanding and truth. Spirituality heals the desire to control and dominate because it fosters greater understanding of life's purpose and your role in life. Consequently, your desire to control events, circumstances and people is replaced with the knowledge that all we need and want will be provided for us in the perfect time in the perfect way as we move through our learning experiences. Life is a learning process. Spirituality is the manner in which we learn and grow.

Another important aspect of spirituality is the recognition and respect of spirit on various levels. Ancestral spirits, nature spirits, and animal spirits must be recognized as they impact on our lives. As we develop spiritual intuitiveness we will be able to communicate and appreciate the impact of these forces. The closer we come to the spirit life, the less violent we become. In the

beginning, however, it is important to simply acknowledge the existence of spirit, and to respect the energy
around us.

Spiritually, we are all teachers and students at the
same time. Once we develop our spirituality, we are able
to recognize our role in any give situation. This recognition gives meaning to our life's experiences beyond those
we sense in our mind or by our emotions. Spiritually, in
any life experience, we are either learning a lesson,
teaching the lesson or the object by which the lesson will
be taught. Once we understand our role, we know our
task. When we know our task, the lesson and the reward
come quickly and easily. —When we are teaching someone a spiritual lesson, we usually have what we call a
negative experience. Someone we love or care about a
great deal will commit an act against us which will violate
a trust or faith we hold. The person will generally make
a choice or decision which seems to be directed to our
detriment. We experience disappointment or emotional
pain. As the teacher, our job may be to assist the person
in seeing the lack of wisdom in their choice. We can best
do this by communicating how we have experienced their
actions. When it is not possible to communicate, we must
simply let go. As a teacher, spirituality requires that we
take action which will benefit everyone involved. Blaming, shaming or laying guilt on the individual will not
assist them in learning the lesson. Communication and
letting go will. Spiritual teachers realize that everything
we think, do and say will return to us in the mirror of self
when the spirit is ready to learn the lesson.—A spiritual
teacher is also the individual who shares spiritual knowledge with you and assists you on your path to spiritual
realization. Often, this can be done without knowledge

on the part of either party. The key is to realize, whoever assists you in becoming a better, more enlightened individual is a spiritual teacher. For adults, our greatest spiritual teachers are our children.—When you are learning a spiritual lesson, you will usually be faced with what we know as a difficult choice or decision. This may occur in a personal relationship or in a worldly experience. The result of the experience, however, will always be the same—you will emerge a more informed person. Some of the more important spiritual lessons we must learn are trust, honesty, forgiveness and patience. In our relationships and experiences we will be faced with situations when we must make a choice to embrace one of these attributes. When we do, we find strength and support. When we do not, we experience or create pain, shame and guilt.—When you are the object by which the spiritual lesson is being taught, you will find yourself in a situation that is not of your own making. Usually two or more people will use you as a pawn, a scapegoat or the object with which they strike out at one another. Children are most usually found in this situation, between their parents. When you are the object by which a lesson is being taught, you must be clear. You must know that the situation is not the result of your choice or your failure to make a choice. You must remain neutral and develop your own relationship with the parties involved, striving to remain neutral. Objects of spiritual lesson must not take sides. They are teaching and learning simultaneously and are therefore in a position of power. The power comes with clarity about what you have to contribute to the situation.—Spirituality requires you to recognize that all experiences in life are purposeful. What you do today, may not have meaning until a later time. However, you must know that nothing happens by chance. You must always seek the deeper meaning to everything that you experience, understanding that the knowledge will bring enlightenment. I once heard a minister say, "If you want to know the purpose of a thing, don't ask the thing, ask the Father of everything." We have the voice of the Father within us. It is the voice of spirit. Spirituality is not "deep" or "mystical" as most of us might imagine. It is probably the most simplistic approach to life. For when you have purpose, you are focused. When you are focused, you have clarity. The role spirit plays in our lives is to make it frighteningly clear to us that we have the power to choose, to know and to be all that we imagine the Creator to be.

Chapter 3

Blessing Your Head

As a child I remember being told that I would never amount to anything. I was constantly reminded about the "bad" things I did. I was always being compared to cousin so and so; the kid next door and other people I didn't even know. I grew up trying to be like everybody else, anybody else other than myself. After all, I was ugly. I was bad. — At first, I wanted to be like Penny, the young blonde cowgirl on the *Sky King* television show. She had long blonde hair and a horse, and everybody liked her. I made home-made pigtails like Penny's by pinning yellow knee socks to my sparse pieces of hair. I would flip them around my head and tell myself how beautiful I was. When they canceled *Sky King*, I decided to be like Veronica in the Archie comic books. Veronica was beautiful and rich but when I realized that nobody liked her, I changed my identity. I decided I was going to be like Mary. No one would dare dislike the mother of Christ.—As luck would have it, there was a big Baptist church directly across the street from my house. I thought Mary would be in all of her glory in that church. I was wrong. The only time she was ever mentioned was at Christmas. I had to find another medium if I was to learn about my mentor. I found it in the Catholic church with my childhood friend Dalilah. —I had my first contact with Mary at St. Matthew's Catholic Church in Brooklyn. She stood as a 12-foot statue with spotlights at the base of her feet. She was positioned in a way that made her eyes follow you everywhere. I was convinced that Mary was looking directly at me. Whether she was or not didn't matter; I knew she would one day speak to me.—I took every opportunity to stop by the church to see Mary. I went after school and on my way to the store. I stopped playing with the other children. I spent many afternoons in long conversations with her. My words were always the same, "Show me how to be like you. Please help me be somebody better." When winter came, I stopped going to church, but I continued my prayer. I'd write letters to Mary and I wrote about her in my diary every day.

One day my older brother and I were having one of our sibling wars. He was screaming at me about being weird and ugly. I was cowering in the corner waiting for him to pounce on me. I took a chance on uncovering my facing to see how close he was to me. When I looked up, I didn't see my brother, I saw Mary. —Mary was standing between my brother and I. Her face was as beautiful as it appeared to be in the church, except she was darker. I realized that Mary, the Mother of Christ, was a Black woman. She was wrapped in flowing blue cloth. Her head was draped in a white cloth which fell across her shoulders. She had a very serious look on her face. I could hear my brother screaming at me, "You make me sick! That's all you ever do! Stop copying what I do!" Then his voice stopped and Mary stared right into my eyes, I felt the touch of her hand on my head and I heard her say, "Just be yourself. "Keep your head clear and be yourself. I will always be with you, in your mind." Then she was gone. My brother was back. I could hear him saying, "Stop trying to be like everybody else!" I just stared at him and started crying.

"Ori," or the head, is the seat of spiritual conscious-ness. As such, we must begin to pay close attention and give great care to the head. We must be conscious and cautious of what we put on and in the head, as well as where we put and what we do with our head. It is through the head, the base of thought, that we are guided. Under-standing spirit as the key to our destiny, we want to keep its house, the head, clear and clean. One way to achieve this is to begin the day with the "Head Blessing Exercise."

In Yoruba culture, we are taught "the head rules the body." We know, with all of the miracle transplants medical science can perform, there is nothing they can do to replace your head. In the New Age thought movement, this theory is represented by the philosophy that whatever is going on in your mind will manifest itself in your life. You give issues, fears and ideas power by virtue of your thoughts. African culture teaches that one must be careful not to speak or think about those things you do not want to see or experience. As one strives to become a spiritual. being, taking time to pray and meditate is the perfect way to keep your head and mind clear. Your head represents a universe within itself. It is round, representing the 360 of knowledge. It is ruled by the astrological sign of Aries. Aries is the concept, "I Am," the power and consciousness of God. Your head is a laboratory through which you take in information and elements, which are then transformed to another state. When you see or hear things, they enter your head, are meshed with your knowledge and experiences and transformed into information that has meaning for you. When you take in food, it is chewed, prepared for digestion by the enzymes in your mouth, and transformed into nourishment which sustains your life. The head also houses your face, which is your universal fingerprint.

In many ancient traditions, people were taught to cover their heads to protect the sacred knowledge they received. In many African cultures, it is considered disrespectful to cover your head during a spiritual ceremony. Africans believe that the spirit enters and leaves the body through the head. Therefore, if the head is covered, you cannot give or receive the blessings of spirit. African Americans today have lost touch with the value and meaning of protecting, blessing and guarding their head. Somehow during the American socialization process, the head has become an item to be adorned rather than an element to be adored. It is through the head that spiritual enrichment takes place. For unless your head and heart are aligned with righteousness, one can never hope to achieve spiritual purification.—As a Yoruba, I have been taught about the sacredness of the head. My godparents, those who initiated me, stressed the importance of following my head, my destiny. My grandmother taught me to always, ". . . follow my first thought," but it was not until I was initiated that I realized the importance of the simple act. What comes into my head is what I need to know. No one else can do or learn what I need to know. Even when I have a negative thought, it is because I have to learn a particular lesson. The same applies to everyone. No one can teach you what you need to learn. You must learn to trust your head. It will never leave you, betray thinking is right?" If you are thinking it, if it will not cause harm to you or anyone else, it is what you are supposed to be thinking. The greatest resistance to our own thoughts is fear. We are taught not to trust ourselves. Consequently, when we have a thought, we do not believe it is good. Because so many of us live in fear, we usually resist what our head tells us to do in lieu of pleasing someone else. Also, our fear of change, failure, the unknown and loneliness allows us to resist the very acts which are necessary for our growth and evolution. One simple way to overcome this challenge is to bless our heads, daily and weekly.

1) You should have a small glass or clay vessel with a cover, which has not been used. Fill the vessel with spring water.

2) Upon arising, before speaking to anyone or beginning daily activities, bless your head with the water in the following manner:

3) Sit or stand in a secluded and quiet area. Place two fingers of each hand into the water.

4) Place fingers in the middle of forehead; draw them from your forehead, across the top and down the back of your head and to the base of your neck.

Prayer: "I bless the spirit of my head."

5) Dip your fingers again. Place your fingers at the top center of your head (the crown). Draw your fingers across your head to your ears. Draw right hand down to right ear. Left hand down to left ear.

Prayer: "I bless the spiritual energy of my head."

6) You will now bless each part of your head in the following order with the appropriate prayer. Dip your fingers before each blessing.

Forehead (Third Eye)
Draw fingers from center of forehead out to each side.
"I bless my spiritual vision that I may see my way clearly."

Eyes
Stroke each eye gently outward. Right hand, right eye, left hand, left eye, simultaneously.
"I bless my eyes that I may see truth in my life."

Nose
Stroke each nostril from top to bottom.
"I bless my breath, enabling my life may be sustained by spirit."

Ears
Stroke each ear with finger tips.
"I bless my ears that I may recognize and follow the guidance of my spirit."

Mouth
Stroke lips from center outward.
"I bless my ability to speak the truth of spirit, to affirm the guidance of spirit; to give thanks for the blessings of spirit."

Face
Stroke the circular outline of your face from the center of the forehead around to your chin.
"I bless my unique identity as an expression of the Creator, making me an expression of divinity."

Bless your head again, from center front to back.
"I bless the spirit of my head to guide me throughout this day."

From center top to either side.

"I bless the spirit of my head to protect me through this day."

You can perform this blessing daily or weekly. If you choose to perform the ceremony weekly, you should give it reinforcement by following steps 1 and 2 daily. Keep your vessel of water covered in places where it is exposed to daylight. Change the water weekly. Feel free to add a sacred oil to the water: Sage for Wisdom; Frankincense for Clarity; Myrrh for Purification. Blessing your head will allow you to begin and end each day by contacting your own spirit, the guiding force in your life.

Chapter 4

Breathing

I was 21 when I first died. My youngest daughter was 6 weeks old. My husband had promised that we would move into a better apartment. We had found a nice little two-bedroom place in a beautiful neighborhood. The rent was affordable and transportation was very accessible. He said he would make all the arrangements. I started packing. I washed all the laundry, threw away all the broken dishes, unhooked the washing machine and promised my children a better life. On the day we were supposed to move, my husband went to the store for bread at 8 a.m. He returned after midnight.

It was a bright Saturday morning. Everything was packed. My husband told me that the moving van would arrive somewhere between 9 and 10 that morning. At 2 p.m. when he had not returned and the truck had not come, I got nervous. I wanted to call, but I didn't know what company he had chosen. I wanted to call the super of the apartment building but I didn't have his number. My mind kept telling me he had lied, but I couldn't accept that. Why would he do this to me? He had taken all the money out of the bank. He told me he signed the lease. He had called the super's number. This couldn't be happening. By 6 p.m., I was in a panic. The baby was crying. The sterilizer was packed. My other children wanted their toys. I couldn't get the box open. The telephone was off. My head was spinning. I couldn't breathe.

I dressed the children and went to the corner telephone booth. I knew the super's last name and the address of the apartment building. He wasn't listed. I kept looking. I found a Winston listed at the address. I called. A woman answered. I babbled my story to her. She gave me the super's number. I called.

'   My name is...."

'   We are supposed to move in today. . ."

'   My husband is working . . . ."

'   The truck hasn't come yet. . . ."

'   What should I do. . . ."

'   Lady, I don't know who you are or what
           you are talking about. . . ."

'   Your husband never came back. . . .

'   I rented the apartment last week. . . ."

'   Lady, Miss . . . , Hello . . ."

It was too late. I was dead.

I kept hearing someone say, "Keep breathing. Just

keep breathing." I couldn't breathe. I was dead. My entire body was numb. I don't know how I got back home. I just sat in the middle of the floor staring at the boxes. I don't know what happened to the baby or the children, I just kept struggling to breathe. Then I saw the box marked "bathroom." I open it. I removed all the pills. One by one I took them all. Tylenol. Aspirin. Phenobaritol. My husband's asthma medication. Vitamins. Water pills. Nightol. I washed it all down with Listerine.

A quiet peace fell over me very slowly. At first I saw brilliant colors. Then I heard music. I saw a man walking towards me. It was my husband. I lashed out at him, biting, kicking, screaming. He pushed me away. I could feel my chest heaving up and down. The voice was back, "Keep breathing. Just keep breathing." I heard the baby crying, but I couldn't see her. Then it hit me, panic. "I'm not breathing! I want to breathe! "Oh God, please help me, I want to breathe!" Then I saw Mary. She reached out to me. I ran to her and fell into her arms. At first I just screamed. Then I cried. When I woke up in the hospital, I was still crying, and I was breathing.

Breathing is the life sustaining exercise which brings the spirit into balance. In the quest for spiritual empowerment and evolution. Breathing must become a conscious function. As we breathe, we strengthen our link to the life force of the Creator. That force provides the means by which we can tap into the very essence of our spiritual nature.

The more conscious we become of our breathing, the more conscious we will be of our connection to the spirit of the Creator. When we have a conscious contact, we can receive enlightenment and information from the depths of our being.

No matter what the circumstances, the instant of death is the same for everyone. We stop breathing. It doesn't matter if we are shot, stabbed, or suffer with a disease. We are alive until we stop breathing. It is through the breath that we stay connected to God. Breath is God's grace, for at any time we can exhale and not inhale. Without breath, the connection to the Creator is broken. The grace of life is removed. In our conscious, awakened state, we have remained connected to the Creator through our breath. As we learn to focus on breath, regulate breath and channel breath, we can focus, regulate and channel the energy of the Creator in our life. It will manifest differently for everyone. It will empower the spirit (Ori) to bring forth the information you need at a given time.

Breath calms the emotions because the emotions we experience do not exist in the Creator. When we experience fear, anger, impatience, hate, we are actually relating to our own experiences and perceptions. These are not characteristics of the Creator. When we experience these emotions, we usually feel out of control. We are in some way threatened. With breath, we can draw on the grace of the Creator and the strength of spirit to guide us. What we usually do is talk, cry or lash out when what we need to do is breathe.

Breath connects the thinking part of us (the masculine energy) to the feeling part of us (the feminine energy). The connection symbolizes a holy union, a force of completion, an experience of joy. Through breath we are made whole and complete. When a man and woman come together, it is an opportunity to create new life. When we connect with our breath, we have the opportunity to create whatever we may need at the moment. We can create strength, peace, power and completion. We can draw on the presence of the divine energy within us. The mind and heart become one and we create a new being. That being comes alive within us. It is actually our ability to transform an experience into something new.

The following exercises are designed to maximize the effects of breath in spiritual development. Whether we are having a negative experience or consciously making contact with spirit, the key is to breathe.

DEEP BREATHING

(Aids in circulation of blood and fosters spiritual cleansing. Also opens ache [power] of the crown and third eye while regulating the heart.)

1) Sit or stand with your back straight.
2) Inhale through your nose as much air as possible.
3) Exhale all of the air through your nose.
4) After exhaling, count to three before inhaling again.
This should be repeated 5-7 times in succession several times throughout the day, particularly before making a decision or responding to an emotional situation.

BALANCING BREATHS

(Aids in spiritual focus and clearing. Opens the ache of the third eye, heart and solar plexus [midriff or seat of balance]. Aids in cleansing lymph glands.)

1) Sit with your back straight and supported if necessary.
2) Cover your right nostril with your left forefinger.
3) Inhale slowly through your left nostril to the count of four.
4) Hold your breath for the count of four.
5) Release the right nostril, cover the left nostril.
6) Exhale slowly to the count of four through the left nostril.

7) Rest to the count of four.
8) Repeat the exercise by covering the left nostril.
9) Inhale through the right, rest.
10) Exhale through the left. Repeat 8 rounds.

After a week or two of persistent daily practice, increase the count to 8 (for inhale, rest, exhale) and the repetitions to 16 twice per day.

CONTINUOUS BREATHS

(Aids in balancing all physical bodily functions.)

1) Inhale as much air as possible through your nose.
2) Without resting, exhale all air through your mouth.
3) Without resting, inhale again, and exhale.
There should be no pulse between inhaling and exhaling. Repeat 10-12 times. This exercise can be done to achieve balance in preparation for any other breathing exercise.

MEDITATIVE BREATHING

(Aids in quieting mind while opening the ache of the crown, heart, third eye and solar plexus. Pulls spiritual energy into crown.)

1) Sit with back straight, feet flat and palms facing upward on thighs and eyes closed.
2) Drop head so that chin is resting on chest.
3) Begin counting mentally while inhaling, rolling head backwards.
4) On the count of seven, head should be hanging backwards. Hold breath 4 counts.
5) Begin counting mentally while rolling head forward and exhaling until chin is resting on chest. Exhale deeply.
6) Repeat exercise four times.

You are now in a meditative state. You may pray mentally. Repeat affirmations or ask your questions. Sit quietly 5-10 minutes.

CLEANSING BREATHS

Sit or stand in a comfortable position.

Inhale through your nose as much air as possible. Exhale through your mouth.

Relax for a few seconds while breathing at a regular pace.

Repeat steps 1,2 3 and 4 for four repetitions.

All breathing exercises should be done consciously. This means you should make the effort to do them. Always keep your back as straight as possible and your shoulders relaxed.

Chapter 5

Meditation

1 saw very little of my father when I was growing up. On those rare occasions when he spent 2 or 3 consecutive days in our household, I came to realize that I was better off with him gone. By the time I was 7 years old, I came to the conclusion that my father was the meanest person alive. No matter what I did or said, my father always addressed me with the same five words, "Sit down! Shut up and listen." At that point, he would give me a 10 minute to 2 hour lecture on the deeper meaning of life; or tooth brushing or shirt ironing or floor sweeping or whatever the issue was at the time.

By the time I was 13, I vowed never to speak to my father for other than the obligatory daily greeting. It didn't matter. If I tried to creep past the living room or bedroom door, he would call me in and give the command, "Sit down! Shut up and listen." He would then tell me about the birds and bees, the birds and dogs, the bird's mother and the bird's father. Ninety-nine percent of the time I had absolutely no idea what my father was saying. It was so philosophical, very intellectual and totally off the wall.

Whenever I had a question or if I offered my childish opinion, he would continue his rambling. I was half asleep when he dismissed me. I knew when the end was near because he always ended the same way, "One day, you'll understand what I'm talking about." That day took 25 years to come.

I was 30 years old when my father made his transition from life. I took it very well because my new-found sense of spirituality helped me understand that life does not end with death. I was 33 years old, well on my way down the path of spiritual enlightenment when I truly understood what my father had said to me. My understanding came when my world fell apart, for the 99th time.

There comes a time in everyone's life when your spiritual philosophy just doesn't seem to answer the questions. This is a desperate moment. You may search for answers which do not seem to come forth. You may read books. They will not make sense. You may ask questions of an elder. Their ramblings will annoy you. My day came when I was verbally attacked by a devout Christian who told me I was going to burn in hell because I had not given my soul to the Lord.

Under normal circumstances this would not have bothered me, but on this particular day, something the woman said just rubbed me the wrong way. I prayed for clarity and guidance. What I got was Jehovah's Witnesses ringing my door bell for three days in a row; Robert Tilton screaming and pointing his finger at me on late-night television; a barrage of religious mail from sources I had never communicated with and a migraine headache. I went walking in the park to think. I sat on a bench to watch the birds. There was an abandoned paper bag begging me to look inside. I did. It was a Bible and a crucifix. I stared at the book in total disbelief when a voice called out to me, "Oh thank God you found it, I thought someone would steal it. You know there are so many evil people on their way to burn in hell." I handed the bag over realizing that my headache had gotten worse.

This went on for two weeks. A myriad of questions kept popping in my mind. Am I doing the right thing? How did the Yoruba faith survive without the Bible? Is there a heaven? Is there a hell? Are African people really condemned to hell because they are Black? What do I believe? I couldn't find the answer. I couldn't sleep at night. I became increasingly irritable. I tried reading my Tarot cards thinking I could get a guage of my emotional level. I pulled the Hanged Man, Death and Fool cards. I checked the calendar to see if the moon was full. There was a new moon, in the sign of Sagittarius—expansion and growth. I was desperate. I took out all my crystals. I laid on the floor and placed the crystals on various parts of my body. They got hot. It felt as though I was on fire. Nothing seemed to work.

Finally I screamed out, "Oh God, please help me! I'm confused! Please tell me what to do!" I was on my knees rocking and crying when the answer came, "Sit down! Shut up and listen!" Those words jarred me back to reality. They came again. "Sit down! Shut up and listen!" I scrambled to a chair. Dried my eyes and waited. Within in few moments my mind was clear. My hands had stopped shaking and it was very clear to me. Each of us vibrates to what our soul knows. An old soul has more experience and a deeper recollection than a young soul. What we believe spiritually is only a reflection of what the soul already recognizes. No one can tell you what is right for your soul because your soul will never forget. Be still and know. What you know in your soul will bring you peace. Be still and listen.

. I had spent hundreds of hours and thousands of dollars buying books, attending workshops and seminars. I had been initiated into orders, societies and faiths. I had slept in the woods; floated in tanks, talked to rocks and stood in fire. All in a search to find what the Father and my father had given me free. I was convinced that I wasn't good enough; that I couldn't do "it" right; there was something that I was missing; and, there was something wrong with me. In the end, I discovered, all I needed to do was shut up and listen. I had to learn how to listen to the quiet voice which spoke from the center of my being. I had to learn that when I didn't know what to say, it was best to say nothing. I had to learn that it did not matter what anyone else was doing or saying, I had to be comfortable within myself. I had to learn that no one can give you what you don't already have. What I had was a soul's experience.

I made it through that growth experience and the many others that followed by taking my father's simple advice. When I don't know what to do, I don't do anything. When I can't figure out what to say, I don't say anything. I stopped letting my ego, the opinions of others and the trend of the times dictate my moods. It took 33 years for me to discover how brilliant my father was. I only hope that he can see how brilliant I have become.

Meditation, while not strictly African, is absolutely spiritual. It is the process of stilling the body and mind to align the physical and spiritual being. The root "medi" like "medicine" means to heal. Meditation brings mental, emotional and spiritual balance, which is the key to enlightenment. It is the process which enables you to contact the true self, eliminating all external interruptions.

Meditation is a process of taking time to do nothing. It is an opportunity to make contact with your spirit and soul. Many of us believe that we don't have time to meditate. The truth is, unless you meditate, you won't have enough time to do what you set out to do. Some of us think we must always be busy doing something. What we fail to realize is, the busier we are, the less we accomplish. Without meditation, we move about frantically and hastily, totally out of control. We are not clear about where we are going, why we are going there and how we are going to get there. Meditation stills the mind, aligns the mind and heart and allows us to transcend time and space.

Meditation should not, cannot be forced. It must be a relaxed, conscious, disciplined effort to focus inward. There are no set rules or procedures which must be followed. However, the meditative process should be consistent and purposeful. You should declare to yourself that you want to meditate and that your goal is either peace, relaxation, enlightenment, etc. You should pick a location in which you feel comfortable and a time in which you will not be disturbed. The key is to practice meditation on a regular basis. As you develop the ability, your spirit will guide you as to what to do next.

The meditative breathing exercise or the simple relaxation meditation is a good place to start. Seated in a comfortable chair, with your back straight, your feet flat on the floor, your palms faced upward, take a deep breath. Close your eyes and relax. If you have trouble relaxing, begin by talking to your body. "My feet are relaxed." "My ankles are relaxed." "My legs are . . .," etc. Talk to every limb and organ from your toes to your head. Believe it or not, that's enough for the first day. Any more will be forcing it. You have just spent 4 - 7 minutes talking to your body. For many of us, that is a first.

The next day try it again. You will probably find it is much easier to relax. So move on to breathing. Listen to yourself breathing. Monitor how long it takes you to inhale and exhale. Next, try to regulate your breathing. Inhale for 4 counts, exhale for 4 counts. Next, inhale 4, hold for 2, exhale for 4. The counting should go on in your head. This means you have totally focused your mind on you. Five minutes should be enough.

On the next day, your goal should be silence. Relax yourself. Regulate your breathing and listen to your thoughts. You may find that a number of things will run through your mind: what you need to do; forgot to do; want to do. You may hear a familiar song or voice. Let these thoughts flow. Your mind is clearing. Your job is to keep negative, disruptive thoughts out. When and if they crop up, simply think, "Peace." Try this process for 3 - 4 days for short intervals until you find that by using the words, "Peace," "Silence," or "Be Still" you can stop the thought.

Finally you will reach a truly meditative readiness. Your goal is to achieve silence. What you will probably hear in your thoughts is the beating of your heart. You will probably feel lightheaded, and be able to sit for longer periods. You may even nod off. It's all fine. You may ask yourself a question and find thoughts answering it. Trust them, it is your spirit speaking. You may get ideas or thoughts about things which seem totally impossible. Act on what you are told and see how it will manifest. You may see things, people or places. That is fine. Once you master quieting your mind, you will find you can meditate while walking or even washing the dishes. Always know that spirit is with you, guiding you and protecting you. Simply relax and let go. Let spirit heal.

Meditation is the process by which you can set aside and let go of the burdens or challenges of your life. It removes you from the past by focusing your attention on now. You cannot realize the calming stillness of the meditative state if you are worrying about the future. Meditate on where you are now. Now means that you must turn your attention within, to the true essence of you. You are divine and meditation permits you to experience your divinity. In your meditative exercises, strive to give yourself time and energy. For it is in this state that your spirit gains ache, power.

Chapter 6

Looking In The Mirror of Self

There is an old saying, "What you draw to you is what you are." For most of us, this is a difficult concept to accept or appreciate. We spend most of our time trying to fix what we see. We try to change people, conditions and situations outside of ourselves because we don't realize that what we are seeing is actually a reflection of who we are. Think of it this way, when you look in the mirror and decide to fix your hair, you don't brush the reflection, you brush the hair on your head. In others words, we have to learn to fix ourselves, not what we see.

A very dear friend of mine taught me this lesson. Over a span of two years, we worked together, confided in one another and worked together to bring our lives into order. At one point our relationship changed and I became her spiritual teacher. At first it felt really great, we had what I thought was a good, honest foundation.

However, as her teacher, my focus shifted. My priority became assisting this woman to grow spiritually. This often meant I had to tell her things that she was resistant to hearing. It also meant that I had to tell her things that I had not yet mastered.

A spiritual brother once told me, "We teach what we most need to learn." Unfortunately, we do not realize we need to learn it and our students have an ego which makes it difficult for them to accept the teacher's weaknesses and flaws. This was the case with my friend. I had revealed to her many of my shortcomings, fears and a past which was not strewn with lilies. She offered support, encouragement and usually a tremendous insight. I respected her and her opinion because, as her teacher, I knew this woman had great potential, as her friend, I understood what her challenges and issues were. What I had not fully come to understand was, who is in our world is a reflection of ourselves. The very things I saw lacking in her were the things I lacked.

From the *Course In Miracles* it is written, "When your brother (sister) acts insanely, it is an opportunity for you to bless him (her). You need the blessing you can offer. There is no way to have it except by giving it . . . Your brother is the mirror in which you see the image of yourself." As usual, I did not understand this statement when I read it. Like most of us, I allowed my ego to convince me that I had it all together. After all, I was a spiritual teacher and counselor. I had helped so many people come to grips with their issues. I was convinced that I had mastered many of the challenges most people struggle to overcome. I had not realized we never stop learning and that a lesson will repeat itself over and over until we recognize it coming. My friend taught me the lesson in a most unpleasant way.

One day, in a spiritual ceremony, my friend acted out. As her teacher, I was forced to take a position. I released her as my student. Her reaction to this was insane. She began writing a series of letters to me. She sent a copy of one letter to everyone she knew, that I knew. She sent the letter to all of my students, my former students, my supervisor at work and the producer of a documentary I had been working on for two years. In the letter, she accused me of being a liar, a thief, and a con artist. She accused me of taking advantage of her, ruining her health and destroying her home. She then wrote about everything I had ever told in confidence as a friend, as justification of her attack on me. My first reaction, I ignored her. My lack of reaction infuriated her, so she started calling people and telling them the story. People then began to question me. I continued to ignore her but somewhere inside of me I knew she was showing me something.

Each of us has something we fear, something we go to all lengths to avoid? Usually it involves ourselves, but it works out as a particular incident or situation. Some people fear animals. Others fear heights or feathers. My fear was not being liked and being talked about. Like Job, my greatest fear had come upon me. People were talking about me. Thinking bad things about me. Questioning me about the validity of my friend's statements. Some people chose to ignore her. Others came to my support and defense. Others assumed it was true because she and I had been so close. I couldn't figure out what to do, so I did nothing. I was hurt. I was angry. I was scared to death. Yet something inside of me was very still. A quiet voice in the back of my mind said, "Just wait for the final outcome and watch who is here when the dust settles." I stopped reading the letters, I stopped answering the telephone. I just watched and waited. I knew the answer would come. I just waited.

When the thing you fear comes upon you, it is like a sharp pain in the pit of your stomach. It causes you to double over. You can't move. And then, it's over. When you don't face your fear, you have a constant ache. You don't know where it comes from or when it is going to stop. You just live with it. Perhaps I am a masochist, but I will take the sharp pain. From one day to the next, my world as I knew it had fallen apart. People doubted the work I was doing. They began to tell their own stories of experiences with me. Most were embellished to fit the story being told, others were down right lies. I wondered what people were saying about me. What were they thinking? How was I going to straighten this out? Were people going to like me? For three weeks the hysteria continued. I knew there was a lesson looming somewhere, but I couldn't see it. Finally, I decided to pray. I asked spirit to show me what was going on. The passage from the *A Course In Miracles* came to me, ". . . your brother is your mirror." It was too painful to look at myself, so I looked at my friend.

My friend feared being abandoned as I had been as a child. She did not want to take responsibility for herself so she blamed others for everything that happened in her life. My friend had low self-esteem and a poor self image. She resented criticism almost as much as I did. My friend was brilliant, intelligent and beautiful, yet, she behaved irrationally, self-destructively and irresponsibly. She did things based on emotions, and then after thinking about what she had done, berated herself. My friend was lonely. She wanted love but was afraid of being hurt or abandoned. She had many painful issues surrounding her worth. She believed people were taking advantage of her. My friend would volunteer to do things for people. When they did not respond a certain way, or pay her what she thought it was worth, she lashed out at the people. My friend said "yes" when she meant "no." She wanted to be liked, needed and accepted. She was, however, convinced, that there was something wrong with her. She thought she wasn't good enough, smart enough and that she did not deserve good things. I knew these things about my friend, but I had not accepted them about myself. I was fixing the mirror. My friend cracked the mirror for me.

Spirit will always give you what you need when you need it. Unfortunately, we don't usually want what we need. We fight tooth and nail by blaming others and refusing to accept the truth about ourselves, we create our own experiences because we need to grow. It was time for me to grow. I had to move to a new level of awareness about myself and my work. It was time for me to let go of thoughts, habits, attitudes, and people which were causing me harm. I had prayed for it. I had asked for it. It came in the only way I was able to accept it at that time— painfully.

The things my friend wrote and said about me were things I had said to myself, about myself. I doubted myself. I questioned myself. I beat up on myself. I believed that my past, my family, and my mistakes made me unworthy. Yet, I projected another image to the world. I spent my time fixing other people; people who I thought did not have it "together." I was fixing the mirror. This experience taught me that whatever we see in others is a reflection of ourself. It was time for me to learn that because a person is defective does not mean they cannot see defects in another. Further, because we are defective does not mean we are not worthy. It simply means we have to work a little harder to learn a little more. In order to be whole, complete and beautiful beings, we have to put the lipstick on our lips, not on the mirror. My friend taught me this lesson in her first letter when she wrote, "... heal yourself and leave the rest of us alone."

The most important step toward the power of spirit is knowing, accepting and loving self. This is a vital process for African-American women. We are the composite of past teachings, past experiences, life pressure and external values. Consequently, it is often difficult to distinguish who we are from what we have been told we are or what we have been taught to be. We are taught to be dependent. We are socialized by generalizations. We are molded through external expectations, most of which are primarily focused on the way we look, the environment from which we come, and the degree to which we attempt to appease the expectations.

Self, true self, is the gentle, knowing, powerful essence of the Creator. Self is without judgment, without societal prejudice, without expectation. Self is the keeper of information and the promoter of revelations. Self is the witness and the judge. Self is the storehouse of guidance necessary to fulfill life's mission. Self is life's student who has studied all that is required to successfully pass life's tests and overcome the obstacles. Since we are taught to respond to life's external stimuli, self is generally the last place we look to find answers, seek guidance or resolve conflict.

When we look in the mirror of self, we are asking to see all that we are, what we have been and what we can be. It is a painful progress; a loving step toward maximum growth and the only way to develop self-acceptance. Looking in the mirror of self opens our eyes to our self-destructive, counterproductive ideas, attitudes and habits. It is the only way to accept responsibility for our actions and the understanding of those experiences. Looking in the mirror of self opens the door to acceptance of mistakes and weaknesses because it crystalizes the quality of our intent. When we can accept what we have done with an understanding of why we acted, we can no longer be persecuted. Looking in the mirror of self reveals the strengths upon which we can rely to guide us through challenges. When we know who we are, accept why we are and understand that we are living to learn, self becomes a constant source of encouragement.

Exercise

1 4-5 foot mirror

2 white candles

1 white sheet or towel

1 straight back chair or floor pillow

You may sit in a chair or in a lotus position on the floor pillow. The room should be completely dark except for the candle light.

1) Place the mirror against a wall so that it is straight.

2) Position the chair or pillow, 3-4 feet directly opposite the mirror.

3) Place one candle on either side of the chair or pillow so that the reflection can be seen in the mirror.

4) Sit with your back flat against the back of the chair or in the lotus position on the pillow, with your back straight.

5) Rest your hands on your knees, palms up.

6) Focus your eyes to a place on the floor in front of the mirror.

7) Take 7-10 deep cleansing breaths and 5 cleansing breaths. Next sit quietly and listen to your breath for a minute or two.

8) Begin repeating in your mind, "I am willing to see my true self."

9) When you can hear your heartbeat in your ears or feel the throbbing throughout your body, slowly raise your eyes to the mirror.

10) Continue repeating the affirmation until your head is straight and you are focused directly on your eyes in the mirror.

11) Take 7-10 deep breaths and 5 cleansing breaths.

12) Begin repeating in your mind, "Show me my real self." When you feel ready, stop the affirmation and concentrate on your breathing. Keep your eyes focused until they feel heavy. When they do, let them close.

What You Can Expect:

- If you see something or someone in the mirror you do not recognize, close your eyes and take cleansing breaths. Re-focus eyes on the floor and raise them slowly again. If the same thing re-appears, stay focused on it, spirit will clarify it for you.

- You may begin to think of an incident or experience from the past. Close your eyes and let it play out. In your mind, ask for understanding and clarity.

- You may begin to have certain thoughts. Listen carefully, ask questions in your mind.

- You may see nothing except the reflection of self. In your mind ask "Who Am I," then listen to your thoughts.

- You may see colors. Check the Color Reference Chart for meaning.

When you feel ready to get up, take a few deep breaths, lower your eyes to the floor, relax your body and move slowly. Write down what you have seen or experienced.

- You can repeat this exercise once a week.

- Do not spend more than 20 minutes for each session.

- This is also an excellent exercise to resolve and gain clarity when you have a conflict with another person. While looking in the mirror ask spirit for clarity and understanding about the situation.

Speaking in the mirror of self is an excellent process for developing positive thoughts which will manifest as conditions in your life. When you can stand in the mirror—look directly into your own eyes and talk to yourself—you command the essence of your being. Your spirit is ready and willing to follow your instructions and commands. The key is to surrender to the energy of spirit as it guides you. When you are speaking to yourself in the mirror, you are opening your mind and spirit to change.

Exercise

Stand before the bathroom mirror in a relaxed posture. Look directly into the reflection of your eyes. Take 3-5 deep, cleansing breaths. In a firm voice, instruct your spirit. The following examples can be used. Feel comfortable to create your own statements.

To Create Wanted Conditions

(Repeat 3, 9 or 21 times.)

"I Am open and willing to change."

"I Am losing weight easily and effortlessly."

"I Am attracting abundantly, positive conditions."

"I Am creating positive conditions/relationships/ situations in my life."

To Create Self Acceptance and Image

"I am beautiful/peaceful/confident/powerful."

"I Am enough."

"I Am worthy just the way I Am."

"I Am that I Am."

Chapter 7

Prayer

One of my spiritual teachers once told me, "When you get tired of struggling, you stop. Then things change." I had become fed up with struggling, suffering and feeling bad. I was truly ready to find out why my life wasn't working. I was extremely talented, but working bored me. I was making money hand over fist and I was still broke. All my relationships ended violently or painfully. I had friends who weren't progressing. Talents I wasn't using. I was in debt, broken-hearted, depressed and angry. Both of my parents were deceased, so I couldn't turn to them. I was forced by the luck of the draw to take a hard, long look at myself.

One of my students recommended that I participate in a Native American purification ceremony, called a "sweat." I had no idea what it was, but she assured me it would help me get in touch with myself. So off I went to the woods, to look at myself and get purified.

A sweat is a process of detoxifying the body, mind and spirit. You are taught how to connect and commune with the earth. Rocks which have been heated on a sacred fire are placed in a pit. The pit is located inside a sacred tent structure called a lodge, which is built to resemble the womb. There were about 20 women "sweating" this day. We filed in one by one and took a seat on the cold bare earth. When the structure is sealed off, it is pitch dark and air tight. Water is then placed on the rocks and steam rises, creating a sauna-like effect in the tent. Sitting with your feet toward the pit of rocks, you pray and sing, allowing the earth to absorb the toxins you are releasing.

My prayer was to release everything that was making my life unhappy. I closed my eyes and began praying. I estimate that it was about 120 degrees in the tent. The heat had a drugging effect. The louder people prayed and sang, the lighter my head became. My eyes were closed but I could see myself. I saw myself exactly as I was dressed, sitting on the earth and hundreds of worms were crawling on me. I jumped and my eyes flew open. I looked down at my hands and legs, there were no worms. I closed my eyes again. This time I was myself as a little girl. It was then the memories began to flood my mind. The abuse. The neglect. The rape. The tears. The loneliness. Scene after scene I could feel the pain of those past experiences. I was crying but I couldn't get my eyes open. The scenes kept coming. The tears were flowing. It was my turn to pray aloud.

After my prayer, everybody was crying. The heat was rising. Somebody wanted to leave, so we prayed for her. When we began singing the healing songs, a cool breeze entered the lodge. I was finally able to open my eyes. Everyone was asked to pray again. This time we all gave thanks for the healing we had received. No one knew exactly what that was, but I for one felt better. When I looked down at the pit of rocks, they all had faces. The faces were smiling at me. The lodge was opened and we began filing out. When the sunlight came into the lodge, I became aware of the hundreds of little pebbles around me. I looked down to see if I had been sitting on any. It was then I saw the piles of dead worms which were laying in the exact spot I had been sitting.

To the African people, prayer is an essential part of each day. The Yoruba believe that it is our duty to begin each day in prayer. Prayer is communion (contact) with the Creator through spirit. It is a method of positive programming of the mind, body and spirit as you seek and give thanks for life and guidance. Daily prayer means that your first contact for the day is with your own Ori (spirit) and the Creator of your Ori. Prayer releases your life force into the universe to produce the right attitudes, reactions and results as you go about your day. Prayer sets into motion the higher laws of mind and spirit.

Every thought you think, every word you speak, is a form of prayer. Why? Thoughts and words are an expression of your life force. When this force is released into the universe, your environment, it will take shape and form. How many times have you said, "You make me sick!" noticing by the end of the day you have a headache, are nauseous or feel exhausted. How many times have you prayed for something good for yourself, realizing, hoping, sometimes wishing, something negative for someone else. Negative thoughts and words cancel out the positive energy of prayer. Careful monitoring of your thoughts and words are required to yield positive prayer results.

Frustration, fear, disappointment, unworthiness, hate, greed, jealousy and self stand in the way of your prayers. Very often when we pray for something, evidence that we cannot or will not get it will manifest in our lives. My grandmother always told me, "Don't believe your lying eyes." If its good for you; if it will not cause harm to you or anyone else; if you believe — it is yours. If you pray for it today, don't pray for the same thing tomorrow. Just give thanks, deny all evidence to the contrary and stand firm.

Prayers are always answered. You don't have to beg or make deals with the Creator when you pray. What you get in answer to your prayer is a direct reflection of what you expect, not necessarily what you pray for. You can pray endlessly and never see the manifestation. The challenge is to pray knowing you will see results. If you pray doubting what you want is possible, you are cancelling out the request. The key is to pray with faith, knowing and believing that what you ask for you already have.

Many people think they do not know how to pray; or, because they are not religious, they cannot/should not pray. This is false. Prayer is an internal experience as well as an external expression. The issue is whether or not you acknowledge that there is something/someone to pray to. If we accept that the life force of the Creator exists within our being, prayer can be seen as communication with the divine part of self. Prayer slows you down, focuses your energy and opens the lines of purification, illumination and union.

Prayer need not be set or fixed in any way. It can be a ritual/ceremony or a brief conversation. The words you choose can be your own or they can be those you have been taught. Since prayer is communion, you should pray what you feel and not what you think. You can pray aloud or to yourself. You can pray standing, sitting, lying or kneeling. The issue is to be humble. You should not fuss or give directions in prayer. You should not express negativity about or towards anything or anyone. You should not make demands or give ultimatums. You should gently express your thoughts or feelings and ask for guidance and clarity about the situation.

Affirmative prayer is a traditional African concept which has been re-affirmed in the New Age. Among the Yoruba, we give prayer by addressing the Creator and our Orisa by their praise names and by citing the marvels they have brought to our life. We call the names of our ancestors who now sit with the Creator and thank them for what they have left us. We thank the natural elements (air, water, fire and earth) for the role they play in sustaining us. We praise the Creator for giving us all that we need and have.

Next, we state our request or dilemma. Speaking about it as clearly and precisely as possible without laying blame, drawing conclusions or making demands. In prayer, it is counterproductive to pray for harm to come to someone, or to ask for anything which will make someone else unhappy. You must ask for the best outcome and claim it by giving praise and thanksgiving. Do not negate your prayers by thinking negative thoughts about what you've asked for. Prayer is like planting a seed. Don't dig it up to see how it is doing. Pray for it. Release it by giving thanks. Begin acting like you already have it.

The concept of praising, requesting and thanking are the components of affirmative prayer. It is a sign of faith that you know the best will come. It is an act of humility in releasing our concerns to the higher forces. If you have nothing to ask for, praise and thanksgiving are enough. If you don't know how to express what you feel, state that and do the best you can. There is no need to make promises, cut deals or make demands. The faith which backs the prayer is the determination of the outcome.

One caution about prayer: be specific in what you ask for and do not pray on the problem. You must pray for the desired solution. A good friend of mine was once without a place to stay. She was sleeping on the floor in a relative's home. Everyday she prayed for a room with a bed. After three months, she found a 6' x 8' room with enough space for a bed and her suitcase. She called me to tell me the good news. After a few minutes of conversation she said, "I know prayer works, so I wonder why I didn't ask for a house."

Prayer is the key—faith unlocks the door. Have faith. You deserve the best. Pray for it, expect it.

It is yours.

PRAYER FOR SPIRITUAL STRENGTH

To the Creator whose mercy endureth
  forever, 1 lift my voice in prayer.

To the Father spirits whose presence
  light my path, 1 lift my mind in
          prayer.

To the Mother spirits whose love is the
  source of my life, 1 lift my spirit in
          prayer.

1 am thankful for the enduring and
  everlasting mercy, light and love in
  in my life.

1 know 1 am watched by protective eyes,
  so 1 can never fall.

1 know 1 am surrounded by unconditional
  love, so 1 am never alone.

1 know 1 am guided by clarity and strength,
  so 1 shall never lose my way.

1 am protected
1 am guided
1 am loved
1 am Thankful.

Chapter 8

Affirmation

"Life and death are in the power of the tongue" (Prov. 18:21). Africans call it Afóse, the power to bring about occurrence by speech. In essence, an affirmation is a statement which declares a situation to be true. It is the bringing forth of the life energy in a concise and positive way and releasing that energy into the universe. Everything we say is an affirmation. It can be positive or negative. The universe does not censor what we say, it simply creates.

My life affirmation was, "It's not going to work." From childhood, I had many experiences which had left me cynical. I didn't believe anything good would ever happen. As a result, it usually didn't. I had a habit of verbalizing what was wrong with everything and every-one. I was always right because that is what I wanted to see. When I began to consciously seek my spirituality, my words took on a new meaning. I would see what I had said almost instantly. Unfortunately it took me awhile to realize what was happening.

My idea of a good relationship was to have a "gorgeous" man. It didn't matter if he was cheap, selfish, confused or a total egomaniac as long as he was gorgeous. He could lie, be unfaithful and unreceptive, but he had to be gorgeous. I always said, "I want a nice-looking man," and that is what I usually got. Unfortunately that's all I got. In the process of seeking the gorgeous man, I usually found fault with myself. I was too fat. I was dark. My legs were skinny. My hair was short and nappy. I had big lips, a flat butt; I had ugly stretch marks. I thought no one would know these things if I had a nice-looking man. Surely no good-looking man would accept these faults in a woman.

I finally met the gorgeous man. Believe me, he was a traffic stopper. I couldn't figure out what he saw in me, but he seemed genuinely interested. My first thought was, "it's not going to work." But each time he called, I convinced myself he accepted me, loved me, wanted me for just being me. I kept struggling with my ideas of inferiority even when they didn't seem to matter to him. I ignored his shortcomings by telling myself it was the best he could do. I accepted the relationship even though I was unhappy with it because I was grateful that this gorgeous man wanted me. What I came to realize was that this man was the instrument being used to bring my words back to me.

A year into the relationship, I decided to express my displeasure with the way things were going. As quietly and gently as I could, I asked this man why we didn't spend more time together. At first he tried to comfort me, but I pushed on. I gave him ideas about things we could do together, places we could go together. He looked at me as though I had grown horns. When I asked him what was wrong, he said, "What makes you think I want to take you anywhere. Do you realize what it would do to my image to be seen somewhere with you!" I asked him what he meant. He went on to talk about my hair, my legs, my weight. He told me how I had been the first "dark skinned" woman he had been with and that I would probably be the last because "we" had too many hangups. In essence this man repeated to me every negative thing I had ever said to myself. When we speak, we may not realize, we are creating. If we say something enough times, we will see it manifest. Often, we do not recognize what we have said when it comes to life. If someone else repeats to us the very thing we have said to ourself, we resist. We feel hurt or angry about the way they have spoken to us. We fail to recognize that they may be repeating the very thing we have said about them or what we have said to ourself. The process of speech creates. It brings the essence of our thoughts and emotions into a tangible form. When we believe what we say and focus our mind on it, it will become truth. It may not be reality, but it will be our truth.

From a spiritual perspective, we can create our reality through speech. The process is called "affirmation." It requires that we use our thoughts and emotions to create what we want and then speak the words which will then manifest as a reality. Affirmations uttered repeatedly create the energy of what we desire and send that energy out to work. They must always be positive, specific and spoken with conviction. The difference between a prayer and an affirmation is purely structural. While prayers are general requests, "Spirit / God give me peace," affirmations are statements of existence "I am peaceful." Affirmations are a back up to prayer since once you request something, the affirmation confirms your belief that it has been given. Affirmations are a positive step toward bringing into your existence all that you need and want.

The language used to develop affirmations determines the effectiveness of the statement. Language which identifies the conditions we do not want, should be avoided.

Ex: "I do not want to be sick."

A more effective affirmation would be, "I am whole and healthy."

Ex: "I do not want to be alone."

Effective Affirmation: "I am one with all life."

Language is the tonal key to the universe. Words create energy. The words we use in our affirmations create energy which will influence the tide of our lives. Structured affirmations create forceful energy. Structure your affirmations to create powerful, focused, positive results, without focusing on the unwanted condition.

Denials

Words which negate the existence of unwanted conditions and beliefs are called denials. They erase negativity as a reality in our lives. Denials pinpoint negativity and issue the command to extinguish it. They serve as the foundation upon which affirmations are built.

Denial: "I am not sick."

Affirmation: "I am whole and healthy."

Every empty space must be filled. When you deny that something can or will exist, you must fill the void with something positive.

Effective Denials and Affirmations

For Centering Energy:

Denial: "I am not confused."

Affirmation: "I am centered in divine clarity and understanding."

Denial: "I am not weak."

Affirmation: "I am strong, peaceful, powerful."

To Attract the Things You Want:

Denial: "There is no lack in my life."

Affirmation: "I am the center of abundance. I am a magnet of prosperity."

When Facing A Major Decision or Challenge:

Denial: "I am not fearful."

Affirmation: "I am facing my challenges with courage and faith."

To Neutralize Energy Between People:

Denial: "There is no disharmony between us."

Affirmation: "I am in perfect harmony with all people and things."

Chapter 9

Forgiving And Releasing

As a child, I spent my summers on Uncle Jimmy's farm in Smithfield, Va. He was a livestock farmer who raised pigs and chickens. During the summer of my eighth birthday, Uncle Jimmy gave me a baby chick. He told me that he would take care of the chick in the winter and I could care for her on my summer visits. Penny grew up to be a beautiful brown and white speckled hen. Uncle Jimmy built a special coop for her so that she wouldn't be sold off as an ordinary chicken.

When I was 10, I made the usual summer journey to Smithfield. I had been there about two weeks when one morning I discovered that Penny was gone. I ran into the house to report the news to Uncle Jimmy and found Aunt Mattie in the kitchen plucking a chicken. I never thought Aunt Mattie liked me and this was all the proof I needed. Aunt Mattie had killed Penny to make soup because, "This cold was killing me and I just grabbed the first old hen I saw!" Surely I didn't want a "sick old aunt" and a "fat healthy hen." When I cried in protest Aunt Mattie screamed at me, "Don't you dare cry over an ole stupid chicken. The yard is full of them! Go get another one."

Uncle Jimmy made her apologize to me and promised to get me a pony. "I'm sure Mattie won't have any use for horse soup." He gave me a dollar for ice cream. I ate three ice cream pops that day and with each one, I vowed never to forgive Aunt Mattie. It took me 24 years to realize how damaging that day had been to me.

Why do we hold on to negativity? For some reason we believe that the other person is affected by our experience. They hurt us and we want to hurt them — we want them to experience our pain, so we hold on. Holding on to pain, anger, guilt, shame or any other negative experience is the glue that binds us to the situation we want to escape.

Each time we encounter a similar situation the memory shifts from the unconscious to the conscious mind. We recreate the initial situation and respond, not to the present, but to the experience we had 5, 10, 20 years prior. Holding onto negative experiences burdens the spirit. It is "an investment in hate, not healing." Spirit, our life force, knows only of the universal law of love, it will not respond to negativity.

Consequently when we hold on to negative emotions, we are denying spirit what it needs to grow and help us grow. The key to opening the way of spirit is "forgiveness."

Everyone is held accountable for what they do, say and even what they think. The responsibility of that accountability, however, is to the Creator. Our life force, spirit, is endowed with the knowledge of universal law, the Creator's law. Those laws mandate that we strive for divine understanding, harmony, peace and love. When spirit is burdened with experiences which are contrary to universal law, the responsibility is on the individual who breaks the law. While the energy of negative thoughts may reach the intended party, the spiritual burden remains on the sender, not on the receiver.

By sending out negative energy, you recreate the negative experience. The person receiving the energy remembers the experience; you recreate the pain; they remember the guilt; you remember the anger. Although you may be thousands of miles apart, you are both locked into the energy of the negative situation. You are not free to move and grow. Forgiveness is the foundation of freedom.

The Creator brings us to the world as unique individuals. We come to this life to learn our own lessons and to complete our unique mission. Often our mission takes us onto the path of others who may have similar lessons to learn. Our lessons come through experiences. How we face and come through those experiences determine our spiritual growth. In every situation, positive or negative, we must try to acertain: Are we learning a lesson? Are we teaching a lesson? Are we the object through which a lesson is being taught? Once we understand our role in any given situation, we can accept our lesson and move on.

Spirit relieves the need to figure out, "Why did this happen to me?" Look for your lesson, or be the willing object of the Creator's work. Spirit has no reason to ask "if" or "what" you did to contribute to the situation. It was a necessary road on your journey. Spirit will not "blame" someone for "doing something" to you. All parties in the experience are teaching or learning. Spirit is indifferent to good or bad. It knows that by universal law we are all held accountable. Spirit is doing its work. We must train our conscious mind to be in harmony with spirit.

Forgiveness is a major step toward spiritual growth and development. It must come from the heart, not the mouth. Forgiveness is the foundation of universal law because it is an effort toward understanding who you are and what your mission is; toward maintaining harmony in the universe and moving in peace—inward and outward. Forgiveness allows us to be free of the negative experiences of anger, pain, disappointment, guilt and shame. When we are free, we are open to experience love, joy, happiness, success and peace. When we forgive, we learn. When we learn we grow—mentally, physically and spiritually.

If you are not receiving good things in your life, you need to forgive. If you are not giving freely and feeling good about it, you need to forgive. If there is anyone you have negative memories about, you need to forgive. If you are feeling lonely, desperate and confused, you need to forgive. Forgiveness is the spiritual laxative, which purges the mind, the heart and the spirit. "The Forgiveness Diet," included in *A Course In Miracles*, is a helpful exercise for releasing past hurts, those you remember and those you do not. It requires a commitment of 20 minutes in the morning, 20 minutes at night, and a brand new notebook.

Select a time in the morning when you will not be disturbed. On a clean page of your notebook, number every other line 1 through 35. Write the following sentence 35 times:

I___(your name)___ forgive _(a person you blame)_

totally and "unconditionally."

Do not pick and choose who you will or will not forgive. Do not think before you write. Write whatever name comes to mind. Try to write 35 different names, however, if one name is repeated, that is fine. When you have completed the exercise, take 5-7 long, deep breaths and close the book.

Repeat the exercise just before you go to bed. This time write the following sentence:

"I ___(your name)___ forgive myself totally and unconditionally. I am free to move on to wholeness and completeness."

You may not know why you need forgiveness. It does not matter. Your spirit will know the reason.

You must repeat this exercise every day, twice a day for 7 days, forgiving others in the A.M. before noon, yourself in the P.M. before midnight. If you miss a day, you must begin again. True forgiveness requires work. Missing a day reflects the resistance of your unconscious mind to releasing the pain. Be gentle with yourself and keep trying. Do not be alarmed if you see or hear from the very person you are forgiving and releasing. Spirit will show you whether you have truly completed your task. Pay attention to how you respond to the situation. When you are forgiven totally you will experience a new sense of freedom.

MEDITATION OF FORGIVENESS

In our deepest hour of need.
The Creator asks for no credentials.
He accepts our flaws.
He is kind and understanding.
He welcomes us because
He knows we are His erring children.
He loves everyone freely and completely
and forgives us for all we have done.
Why can't we forgive ourselves?

Unknown

Chapter 10

Ritual

Every morning, my grandmother would get up, wash up, make a pot of coffee, place a chair in front of the kitchen window and read from a small frayed black book. By 7 a.m., she was fully dressed, breakfast was ready and my clothes were laid out for me to wear. I was expected to get up, make my bed and be washed by 7:15. We were blessing our breakfast by 7:30 a.m.

Every Monday we washed the crystal and polished the silver. On Tuesday and Thursday, we took Father John's and castor oil. Every Thursday we washed our clothes, by hand, on a scrub board. Every Saturday morning, we sprinkled the dry, starched clothes, rolled them, placed them in the refrigerator, to be ironed Saturday evening. We went to Sunday school and church every Sunday. We ate dinner every weeknight at 5:30. On Sunday we ate at 3:30. I lived by granny's strict schedule for the first 16 years of my life. At 16, I decided to do it differently.

My grandmother paid her bills on time. She never had a toothache, I don't remember that she ever had a cold. There was no dust in granny's house, her plants never died. My grandmother didn't know the exact date or year of her birth. She never went to school. Widowed at age 15, she never remarried. She had only one child, my father, and she never grew hair on her chin. In 1990, we quessed our grandmother was 92 years old. She lives alone, in Virginia, has full control of her faculties and bodily functions. She has never read a book, but can quote the Bible and the almanac. Granny can't spell meditation, yet she does it everyday. She has never been to a workshop or a retreat, but I know, my grandmother has a direct line to the Creator.

At age 16, I discovered boys and fun. I rebelled against my granny's schedule. At age 17, I had my first child. At age 19, I entered an abusive marriage. At 22, I had my first nervous breakdown. My grandmother did not visit me in the hospital. I never called her when I was released. At age 23, I began receiving public assistance. At age 25, I was virtually homeless. At age 29, I was in therapy. When I was 30, my husband broke my jaw, I had my second breakdown, my first breakthrough and a long talk with granny.

Grandma told me the importance of doing things on time. She called it, "following God's clock." Granny explained how the clock worked. The sunlight of the day is the best time to do the things that support life. The darkness is the time to restore and make medicine. Spring is the time of new growth and fresh starts. Summer is the time that will bring the benefits of what was done in the spring. Fall is the time of death, time to eliminate the old. the worn out, the useless. Always leave your bad relationships in the fall. Winter is the time to rest, plan and rejuvenate. Grandma said that the sun is the man's energy, the energy that supports life. The moon is the woman's energy, the energy in which life is created.

My grandmother talked about the phases of the moon and the energies of the months. She said, "God has given us a clock. The same thing happens, at the same time, year in and year out. If you follow God's clock, you will always be on time and you will get better at what you do. You never have to wonder about what's going to happen when you follow the natural clock, you already know. You can have a schedule if you like, but, remember who owns the clock." What grandma called "the clock," is what African people call ritual.

A ritual is a prescribed way of performing an act or certain acts. A ritual is the traditional or ceremonial approach to an event or series of events. African people are a ritualistic people. Tradition mandates that African people approach life events and actions ritually. Our ancestral cultures prescribes secret rituals, religious rituals, social rituals, family rituals and personal rituals. These rituals create, utilize and release energy. They demand and create sacredness.

In your journey toward spiritual evolution, develop a ritualistic approach to your exercises. This means you should approach them the same way, the same time in the same place as often as you can. Set realistic goals based on your circumstances and schedule. Begin by setting a time limit. Ten-twenty minutes is a good place to start. Make a commitment to a certain number of days. Select a location where you feel comfortable and will not be disturbed, for the allotted time. Inform your family and loved ones not to disturb you during this time. This will elicit their support and respect of your time, as well as destroy your excuses not to continue, which are bound to arise as you attempt to discipline your mind.

If you have a special chair, garment or other instruments you will use for your ritual, try not to use them at any other time. This will instill and preserve their sacredness. If you miss a committed time, do not be angry or distressed. Continue your activity at the next scheduled time. Feel free to perform your ritual at any additional time as you feel necessary. In any case, you should make every attempt to continue your ritual for three months consistently before you amend it, unless you are directed by spirit to do so. Consistent practice helps to develop discipline, which is a key element of spirituality. The following beginners ritual may prove helpful for actual practice or as a guide for developing your own spiritual ritual.

Practice Sunday, Tuesday, and Thursday for a 90-day period before any other daily activity. After your evening bath, repeat this exercise.

1. Arise 30 minutes earlier than regular.

2. Draw water and perform Head Blessing Ritual.

3. Eight repetitions of deep breathing. Pray for self, family, community. Ask 3 questions about challenges or situations you are facing. (The same question may be repeated on 7 different occasions if the answer is not immediately apparent).

4. Four repetitions of meditative breathing.

5. Spend 5-10 minutes in silence. You need not

check a watch or clock. Ask your spirit to make you aware when 5 minutes has passed. You will be alerted by a sound or feeling.

6. Four repetitions of circular breaths before leaving ritual area.

7. Repeat the entire exercise before retiring.

Chapter 11

Altars

A shrine is an area of consecrated energy and a place for sacred rituals. Shrines are a principal element of African culture. The pyramids are ancient African shrines. Totems are shrines among the Native Americans. The Washington Monument is a shrine among Anglo-Americans. Unfortunately, African descendants have been limited and imprisoned by the English language. Consequently, we are uncomfortable with and turned off by certain words.

In our industrialized, computerized society, we are uncomfortable with shrines, so we have altars. As you will, an altar is an area of consecrated energy and a place for sacred rituals. An altar is a principle element of spiritual development in that it supplies a visual and physical focus for your energy and activity. An altar is necessary only to the point that it enables you to focus your mind, house your sacred implements and provide a consecrated location for your spiritual ritual.

An altar may be as simple or elaborate as will meet

your needs and tastes. There are, however, certain "shoulds" to be practiced if you are going to set up an altar.

1. Cover your foundation (e.g., table, case, etc.) with a white cloth. This alerts spirit that you are seeking light and clarity.

2. Place your altar in a place which is not heavily trafficked by daily family activities. An empty closet serves adequately for apartment dwellers. If you own or live in a home, try a secluded area of the attic or basement.

3. Cleanse and consecrate the area in which your altar will be. Cleanse first by washing, sweeping and mopping the area. This can be done with detergent followed by a herbal washing. Sage, rosemary or hyssop boiled and strained makes an excellent herbal cleanser.

You may also add essential rose, myrrh or frankincense oil to the water while boiling. After washing you can "smoke" the area out with incense.

4. Do not use the area for any other activity other than your spiritual exercises. (e.g., meditation, prayer).

5. You may place on your altar only those implements which are necessary for your spiritual exercises, and they should be consecrated.

Remember, you are a divine expression of the Creator. You have the ability and the right to consecrated implements for your sacred use. You may do this by cleansing the item and praying over it, recognizing its sacred energy and decreeing it suitable for your sacred use.

There are certain elements and implements which prove beneficial for use on an altar.

1) One, seven, or nine glasses of water.

2) Candle or other form of light.

3) Symbol of divinity, e.g., a cross or ankh.

Ancestral Altar

This particular altar should be set up on the floor because ancestral spirits provide grounding. The altar area should be encircled with white chalk with 9 lines drawn across the circle. Within the circle the following items should be placed:

1 - Pictures of deceased family members.

2 - Hats, pipes, canes or other memorabilia of family members.

3 - Vessel of water (for purification)

4 - Cup of coffee (staple product of earth).

5 - Small glass of honey.

6 - Small glass of molasses.

7 - Small glass of milk.

8 - 2 glass-enclosed white candles on both sides of circle.

9 - Small bottles of liquor (any particular brand family members enjoyed, however, white rum or gin must be included. Liquor represents an element which has gone through several processes before completion).

10 - Cigar, to be lit and placed over coffee cup (tobacco is the sacred herb of the earth).

You can also put cloth dolls or masks within the circle to represent ancestral forces.

When burning incense to invoke the ancestral forces, the following blends are particularly pleasing:

Frankincense & Myrrh—Strength, Purification, Power

Rosemary & Lavender—Purification, Love

Anise Seeds & Rosemary—Spiritual Clarity and Purification

Lavender & Cinnamon Sticks—Love

Sage, Rosemary & Lavender Buds—Purification, Wisdom, & Love

Rose or Sandalwood Cones—Love & Prosperity

It is best to use fresh herbs on a charcoal block or pure incense sticks.

Spiritual Development Altar

Water is the medium of spiritual purification. It is the element through which spiritual energy passes clearly and effectively. Water on the spiritual altar fosters clear, effective and pure spiritual communication. If one glass or vessel of water is used, it is dedicated to the divine energy of spirit.

Seven glasses of water are to be dedicated to the spiritual forces which surround every individual.

1) Spirit of your head

2) Spirit of your parents (whether living or deceased) and Spirit of your ancestors (known and unknown)

who have made you who you are

3) Spirit of masculine energy

4) Spirit of feminine energy

5) Spirit of child

6) Karmic Spirit (any spiritual energy from past existences)   *

7) Spirit of the Creator, the Godhead which supports the divinity of your existence.

3)		6)	* It is helpful when
2)	7*	5)	this glass or vessel
1)		4)	is larger than the other 6 glasses.

Each vessel of water should be consecrated in the following manner:

Hold the vessel on the top of your head and recite the following prayer:

"I dedicate this water to _____ (Fill in one of the spiritual energies listed—your head, your parents and ancestors, masculine energy, etc. One glass should be dedicated for each energy). I dedicate this water for your purification, elevation and evolution. I dedicate this water so that the spirit of _____ will provide me spiritual assistance, spiritual strength, spiritual clarity and spiritual understanding. I dedicate this water for my spiritual growth."

The final vessel of water to be presented is the God-head which will seal the table in light and divinity. The above prayer, as well as your personal favorite, may be recited. You can also dedicate this glass with a special prayer for yourself. Once this glass is placed on the table, you can light a candle and begin your spiritual exercise.

The water should be changed at least once per week. Each time you change the water you must re-dedicate the glasses to the spiritual force they represent. In the beginning you may notice tiny bubbles filling the surface of the glass. This indicates that the spiritual forces are drawing and cleansing energy from you and your environment. It is fine. The clearer the water becomes, the clearer you will be. You can add a pinch of alum to the 6 primary glasses to intensify the vibrations. A few drops of mercury in the center glass will do the same.

Understand that in the absence of traditional shrines and in the environment in which we live an altar is a spiritual aid. It is not strictly African nor is it absolutely Anglo-American. An altar is an expression of spirituality resulting from the evolutionary process experienced by the African American.

Finally, please note that the above description relates to an individual altar for spiritual development. It is not an ancestral altar. An ancestral altar should be set up on the floor or on the earth. The minimum require-ments have been discussed here. If you feel the need or desire to consecrate a more modest or elaborate ancestral altar, ask your spirit in prayer and meditation for guidance and instruction. Follow those instructions implicitly.

ANCESTRAL ALTAR

SPIRITUAL DEVELOPMENT ALTAR

GUARDIAN SPIRIT ALTAR

Chapter 12

Spiritual Bathing

When she open the door, I fought to stifle a scream. Her skin was as black as coal. Her eyes were piercingly white. So white, I could see them through the black lens of the sunglasses. Her head was wrapped in what appeared to be a red bed sheet. The piles of cloth on her head matched her long red dress. The ruffled dress resembled the style of the old television mammies, complete with a red and white checkered apron. The 12-inch cross around her neck hung from a thin piece of clothesline. "Mother Mary?" She never answered. She told me to step back from the door, walk down the stairs and wait at the basement door. She slammed the door in my face before I could move. Obediently, I walked down the steps to the door. A small voice in my brain was laughing hysterically when the door flew open. Before I could say a word, Mother Mary threw a bucket of ice cold water in my face. I stood there dripping wet, trying to catch my breath. "Come on in sweetheart."

I stepped through the doorway saying a silent prayer,

"Dear God, when am I going to learn. "

As I sat shivering, Mother listened intently to my story. No money. Trying to finish school. Bad relationship. Can't eat. Can't sleep. Mother sick. Losing my mind. Father could care less. Mother's eyes seemed to be piercing my skin as she stared at me. She was fondling the cross when she finally said, "The devil hates the cold you know." She stood up and walked away.

She had left me in a basement room which resembled a church. There was an ancient piano, chairs set up auditorium style, a cross on every wall and a stack of hymnals on the floor.

"The devil likes Black people." She was yelling out from the other room.

"He is particularly fond of Black women. You know why?"

"No, why?"

"Because they're weak."

My political intelligence was immediately offended.

"They've been weak every since the old African mothers stopped teaching about God and His medicine. They been weak since they straightened their hair and put on panty girdles. They weak cause they sleep in them big, fat pink hair rollers. God can't talk through hair rollers you know." I thought to myself, "Oh God, what am I doing in this basement with this crazy woman?"

Mother called out, "Come to me sweetheart." I laid my wet coat on a chair and walked into the other room. Mother was standing beside a shower stall. She had a

white plate in her hands. Quickly I scanned the bathroom. There was a glass encased candle on a shelf in
every corner. To my left, there was a shelf with 6 or 7
candles of different colors, with a picture of a saint next to
each one. There was a sweet-smelling smoke swirling
around behind Mother which made her seem like an
apparition. On the wall directly in front of me, above
Mother's head, was a huge poster of the Virgin Mary. Just
like the vision I had so many years before, the Virgin was
a beautiful Black woman.

Mother told me to kneel down. She placed the plate
on top of my head and started singing. She was singing so
loud and off key, I was embarrassed. She started praying.
She was calling the names of people I didn't know. In the
process, she called my father, Horace, and my mother,
Sarah. That wiped the embarrassed smirk right off my
face. Now she was speaking in a language I couldn't
understand. Somebody understood her, because they
answered her. I heard two distinct voices. One male.
One female. Both loud. I didn't dare open my eyes.

"Get in the tub." Who was she talking to? This time
she screamed, "Get Up! Get in the tub!" Scrambling to my
feet, I half stepped, half fell into the shower stall.

"Put your hands on the wall! Spread your legs apart!"

Obediently I followed orders as I thought to myself,
"Please don't let her kill me." I felt her hands ripping at my
clothes. One yank, my $30 sweater was gone. Ripping.
Tearing. The skirt fell off. Now the scissors. Bra first.
Panties next. The yanking at the pantyhose almost spun
me around.

"Face the wall! Don't look back! Don't ever look

back!"

My toes gripped at the floor tile as my fingers gripped the walls. The first blow came to the top of my head.

She was singing some crazy-sounding song as she washed my body with eggs. From the top off my head, across my face, down my back to my legs. I could feel the egg shells cutting my skin. I couldn't open my eyes. I tucked my lips in to avoid the taste of the raw eggs. Abruptly she stopped. I could hear her step away. She was praying again.

Without warning, Mother doused me with another bucket of water. She started scrubbing me down, then she handed me her tools. Lemons.

"Wash your face and your privates"

As I washed, she poured. Ice cold water.

"Stomp on those clothes"

I was shivering, stomping, scrubbing myself with the lemon rinds.

"Jump on those clothes! Stomp it out."

I jumped, shivering and scrubbing. It was a frenzied experience.

"Tell him to get back!" Mother gave me a whack on the bottom.

" Tell him to leave you alone." I don't know what Mother had in the water, or, who "He" was, but I was screaming at him. "Leave me alone." I was stomping and screaming. Shivering and screaming. Scrubbing and screaming. Mother gave me more lemons. I was frantic.

I scrubbed my arms. Legs. Face. Under my breast and my privates. I was screaming at the top of my lungs when I heard Mother's calm melodic voice, "Now don't hurt yourself baby. It's gone."

When I fell to my knees in the stall, Mother was ready with another bucket of water. This time the water was warm and sweet-smelling. Gently she stroked my body to remove the egg shells and lemon rinds. She was humming now. "You got a change of clothes?" I shook my head no. Mother walked away, leaving me exhausted on the shower stall floor. I heard her go up and come back down the stairs. "Put this on, but don't dry your body." I got dressed.

When I came out of the bathroom, Mother just stared at me.

"Now don't go feelin' ashamed because your breast hang! Any breast that nursed babies is supposed to hang."

I was wearing a parrot-green crochet knit sweater and a red skirt that was four inches over my knees. My brown ankle boots were soaking wet from the first drowning. "You look much better. You are such a beautiful woman. I don't know why you let people make you feel ugly." I didn't even care how she knew. I felt 100% better. Lightheaded but better.

Mother took my hands and prayed with me. She told me to go home and be good to myself. Mother told me that God had given me special blessings. My problem was, I didn't realize how specially blessed I was. Mother kissed my forehead. She told me that her work was free, but, when I could, send $250 to the post office box. The church needed my support. I picked up my dripping wet, wrinkled coat, threw it over my arm and headed for the door. Mother called out to me, "Eggs are sacred forces of life. Lemons cut bitterness. When in doubt, just get in the water." I told her thank you and left.

As the source of life, water is the most powerful healing force ever known to man. All natural sources of water house the "mother force" of the universe. Water soothes, heals, nurtures and cleanses. Water the warrior, the protector, is always available. If you cannot get to a river, a lake or the ocean, you can always immerse yourself in the bathtub. The energy of water changes your consciousness and helps to move energy. Water nurtures your being because it is symbolic of the protection of the womb.

Talking, praying, affirming your desires in or over water is a powerful way to put the universe on notice that you are in need. Sprinkle perfumed water around the house to create a clearing and refreshing energy. Place a clear glass of water under the head of your bed to remove cloudy energy that may be blocking your memory of dreams. Keep large vessels of water around the house to draw and clear negative energy. Drink plenty of water daily to keep your system flushed. Water is the mother of life, keep that energy alive.

To give water an extra healing effect you can add a few drops of an essential oil or a handful of herbs to your bath water. Oils provide stimulation to the central nervous system and the spiritual centers (ache). Herbs create a vibratory energy force around the physical body and attract similar energy from the universe. Both herbs and oils have a healing affect on the mind and body. They should be used in hot water.

SPIRITUAL BATHING

OILS	USED FOR	*HERBS*	USED FOR
ROSE	Depression Insomnia Uterine Disorders Peace	SAGE	Mental
		CHAMOMILE	Clarity
LAVENDER	Tension, Self-hate, Fear, Creativity	COMFREY	Relaxation Spiritual Vision
JASMINE	Frigidity, Impotence, Depression, Confusion, Spiritual, Attraction	LAVENDER BUDS	Self Love, Creativity
		ROSE BUDS (PINK) ROSE BUDS (RED)	Universal Love, Protection Passion, Lust
BASIL	Colds, Earache, Mental Fatigue		
MYRRH	Fear, Anger, Fatigue, Confusion	ROSEMARY	Spiritual Purification

OILS	USED FOR	HERBS	USED FOR
ORANGE BLOSSOM	Tension, Heart Palpitations, Insomnia	JASMINE	Clear Emotions
		MINTS	Prosperity
PEPPERMINT	Colds, Metal Fatigue, Asthma	HYSSOP	Spiritual, Clarity, Purification
SANDALWOOD	Nausea, Tension	LEMON	Spiritual Purification
MARIGOLD	Grief, Loss		
ROSEMARY	Memory Lapse Fatigue, Purification		
HONEY SUCKLE	Prosperity		

Chapter 13

Help From The Planet Earth

The Convent for the Order of the Holy Mother is located in a small suburban town, 60 miles outside of Detroit. Over 250 acres of land, which housed a small lake, a corn field and every type of tree imaginable, is not what I thought a convent would look like. It was beautiful. It was serene. It was an ideal location for house-searching Black women on spiritual retreat. At first I felt a little uncomfortable going to a convent. I wasn't a Christian. Most nuns are white. I still had a tendency to use four-letter words. And, where was I going to smoke? Once I set foot on the property, I knew that something miraculous was about to take place.

It was early Saturday morning when my spiritual sister and I began the workshops. Creating a New Reality. That was our goal. For 6 hours, Shaheerah and I taught about the power of the mind. The value of the spirit and the wisdom of God. We conducted meditations, visualization and soul-freeing exercises. A mother who had not spoken to her son in six years came to realize that she would see him again. A woman who had never spoken in public stood up and gave a 10-minute speech about the pain in her life. A woman who had come to the retreat by mistake, knew no one in the group, decided to stay. One by one, people began to realize their beauty, their power, their connection to the Creator. We cried about it. We sang about it. We made a miracle scorecard. At the end of the first session we had chalked up 15 miracles. It was time for dinner.

I decided to take a walk. It was a beautiful day. The grass was freshly cut. The pine, oak and elm trees offered shade from the sun. The energy was flowing through my body at 75 miles an hour. I needed to be grounded. Get centered. I walked to a large open field where the earth seemed to meet the sky. I laid on the ground in spread-eagle fashion and began to pray. I had been laying there for about 10 minutes when I realized I wasn't alone. There seemed to be a misty fog hovering over me. There was a sweet smell in the air and a cool breeze. I wanted to open my eyes but I couldn't. Suddenly my stomach did a somersault as if I had just gone down the first hill of a roller coaster. The fog became denser and I could feel it on my skin. Now I was scared.

As I began to breathe deeper, I heard the voice, "What do you want?" It was a heavy, deeply male voice. It was gentle but stern. My mind was fuzzy. I couldn't figure out if I was asleep or awake. I could feel the sun shinning on my skin and although my eyes were closed, I could see the fog. I heard it again. "What do you want?" "Oh, shit, God is talking to me!" I knew I had gone over the deep end. Then I felt bad for cursing. Suppose it really is God? Now I've cursed at him. But why would God be talking to me? I don't believe this shit! God is talking to me! The smell was lingering under my nose. I could hear my heart pounding in my ears. My eyes were closed but I could see everything. I wanted to turn my head to actually see but I couldn't move. "You're crazy," I told myself. Then I heard myself saying, "God is talking to you." Then the voice came again. This time it was louder, firmer and right in my ear, "What is it that you want."

My mind was blank and flooding at the same time. What are you supposed to say when God asks you what you want. All of the spiritual theory went right out the window. I was struggling to figure out what was happening. All of my self value and worth issues were staring me in the face. Why would God take the time to talk to me? Here I was, a lowly human, trying to do my spiritual work, struggling with my own issues and God Himself was talking to me. How did I know this was real? Somehow, I just knew it and it scared me to death.

Did I ask God for a cure for AIDS? No. Did I ask God for the secret to a wholesome, prosperous life? No. Did I ask Him to eradicate poverty? Racism? The abuse of women and children? No. I had been praying for more than 30 years for all the things I thought were politically and spiritually correct. I had asked for clarity, guidance and understanding. I had children who needed protection. Friends who needed help. Clients who needed salvation. When the voice came for the fourth time, "What do you want?" I responded, "A car."

I was embarrassed for myself. How could I waste this glorious opportunity. As soon as the words were out of my mouth, everything became frightening still. I thought I was dead, but the voice came back, "What do you believe about a car?" Oh God, now what do I say. The words rolled off my tongue, "I believe you need money to get a car." "You don't need money to get a car. All you need is an idea. A car is simply an idea in your mind. Your mind is in My mind. All I do is create ideas. You bring my ideas into the world." I couldn't speak. The voice came back, "If you keep you mind stayed on My mind, you can have anything because every thing are my ideas. You are an idea in my mind. You belong to me." On a very deep level of my being it all made sense. If God is the source of all life, everyone and everything belongs to God. The thought crossed my mind, "Well, how come we can't get things together?" The answer came quickly, "Your ego and will send you on a search for things you already have. Still your ego and keep your mind on me." The fog lifted. My eyes opened. I knew it was real.

I sat up slowly trying to make sense of it. The earth beneath me felt alive. I could feel it pulsing. The trees seemed to be watching me. There were several birds walking within 12 inches of me. I could hear the sound of a waterfall that I could see. I tried to stand up. I was floating. I could smell the flowers. It seemed as though I could see for miles. I felt a peace and stillness within myself that I could not explain. When I finally stood up and turned around, I noticed a 20-foot marble statue of the Virgin Mary. She was looking directly at me. My heart jumped. I shut my eyes. When I opened them, the statue was gone. Six months later, with a $37,000 student loan in default, an overdrawn bank account and $15 in a savings account, I was given the title and keys to a new car.

The Creator has placed at our disposal a wealth of natural energies that are willing and useful healing tools.

We need only ask and the help is there for us.

TREES

These mighty friends are elemental symbols of wisdom. There are tangible signs of transformation and growth. Trees are receptive and energizing. They stand as symbols and representation of our endless source of supply. We can talk to trees, particularly elms and oaks. Weeping willows are eager receptacles for our sorrows — they take our tears and transform them into beauty.

An excellent clearing ritual can be performed at the foot of a tree. Dig a small hole in front of the tree or near the roots. Lie flat on the earth and talk directly into the hole. Talk as though you were speaking to a person. If you are expressing pain, sorrow, fear, etc., tell the tree exactly what the cause is and how you feel about it. If you are making a request, be specific. Talk about the situation, what you feel and propose an outcome. When you have fully expressed yourself, re-cover the hole. Thank the tree and leave an offering—pennies, a flower, fruit. Ask the tree to take your concerns and turn them into something beautiful. The simple way is to simply sit on the ground with your back against the tree and talk it out. Always leave an offering. In essence you are paying for the work the tree will do.

RIVERS

Rivers are the sweet waters of the universe. Re–presenting the energy of Venus, they hold the powers of love, wealth, community consciousness and emotional well being. Rivers attend to the day to day flow of life; how we respond to it and how we can overcome the challenges we encounter.

Sitting at the river bank, talking aloud about your emotions, is an excellent cleansing ritual. Releasing and clearing emotions about relationships should be done at the river. Prayers for information, direction and guidance should be made at the river. When praying/meditating at the river, it is advisable to ring a small brass bell. When you are done, leave an offering of honey, yellow flowers, 5 pennies, nickles or dimes. Never throw garbage into or leave it at the river bank.

Note: The honey can be poured into the river while you are ringing the bell and praying.

OCEAN

The ocean is the ultimate "Mother Force" of the universe. Like the amniotic fluid which nurtures life, the ocean is a supportive, protective, nurturing and healing energy. You can take all of your troubles to "Mother"— she is an enduring source of strength.

Like all mothers, the ocean energy is primarily concerned with health. For us, that translates to mental, physical and spiritual health. Meditation and prayer at the ocean is one of the most powerful and effective healing tools at our disposal. The ocean is littered with the bodies and spiritual energy of African ancestors. They live because the ocean supports life in many forms. When you go to the ocean, be humble and respectful. Do not wear shoes, fancy clothing or make-up. Always take an offering of fruit, molasses, blue cloth or silver coins. Make your prayer with outstretched arms. Leave your offering at the water's edge.

The ocean is the best place to cry. (The river will take your tears and sweeten them also.) When you cry at the ocean, "Mother" will wash away the source of your tears. Be very mindful of what you ask for at the oceanside and if you recognize people, conditions and situations leaving your life, do not pull them back to you.

MOUNTAINS

If you want peace, mental clarity, tranquility and understanding, go alone to the mountain top. When you want to forgive or be forgiven, dress in white and go to the mountain top. For evolution, quick resolutions and instant illumination go to the mountain top, for it is there that the Father resides.

Take a single coconut, hold it in the center of your forehead, make your prayer aloud. Place the coconut in a well-nestled place and leave it. Spend 20-30 minutes in silence, eyes closed, with the palms of the hands turned upwards. End your prayer/meditation with joyous thanksgiving. Never tell anyone what you've asked for and never ask for it again. Mountain energy is a slow energy, however, it is the most definite energy available.

FIRE

Fire creates the direct link of communication between man and the Creator. It is a cleansing, consistent and powerful way of releasing energy into the universe. Fire carries a vibratory effect which permeates all levels of the universe. It lends illumination on the spiritual level and consistency on the physical level. Our source of fire is the use of candles.

Candles add a vibration to the prayers we offer and requests we make. The body of the candle holds the thoughts, the fire sends it into the universe. The color of the candle provides the energy we want to create. The flame carries that energy upward and outward. Candles are strongly recommend for those of us who lack the discipline to repeat the same prayer/affirmations daily as well as those of us whose faith is strong enough to ask for it once and let it go.

The greatest success may come from the use of a "pull-out" 7-day candle. The wax body of the candle can be held during prayer, then replaced in the glass.

Your thoughts, your energy are captured by the wax and released as the candle burns down. As with anything spiritual, you get out of it what you put into it. When "charging" your candle, be relaxed, be clear, be positive.

(Note: Always keep a lit candle in an open, stable location. The higher the better. Place it in a saucer or bowl of water.)

Select the color of candle which vibrates the level of energy you wish to attract. (See below.)

COLOR
The vibratory effects of color emit energy and influence on the mind and emotions. Color sends a message into the universe and draws upon the energies of the universe. The decor of our homes, the clothes we wear, even the food we eat carry the vibratory effects of color. We can create and dispel energy by the clothes we wear because they radiate the energy of our being. Choose your colors carefully, attuned to what you feel or what you desire to draw to you.

COLOR—VIBRATORY PRINCIPLE *

Red - Passion, Courage, Anger, Greed, Lust.

Orange - Energy, Dynamic Force, Fertility, Pride.

Yellow - Mind, Intellect, Optimism, Forgiveness, Vision.

Green - Prosperity, Success, Versatility, Supply, Independence.

Blue - Inspiration, Religion, Devotion, Healing, Artistic Ability.

Purple - High Spirit, Holy, Divine Radiance.

Grey - Formality, Lack of Imagination, Fear.

Brown - Depression, Stagnation, Practicality.

Pink - Universal Love, Tenderness, Frailty.

White - Clarity, Innocence, Wisdom, Strength.

Black - Reversing, Draws All Forces, Emits None.

* The richer and deeper the tone, the stronger the vibration of the color.

Chapter 14

Spiritual Code Of Conduct

When I first heard the term, "Talk the talk and walk the walk," I really thought I knew what it meant. Of course I didn't. I had built my spiritual foundation on self-deception. I was doing all the right things, praying the right prayers, putting forth the right image. Inside, I was still avoiding myself, blaming others for my shortcomings and using my spiritual knowledge as an escape. I still had fears. I still hated my father. I was not living up to my full potential and I told lies. Everything was going great.

I really believed I had sufficiently covered my weaknesses. I thought if I continued reading books, going to workshops, saying the right things to the right people, everyone would know how wonderful I was. I made one deadly error. In an earnest prayer, I asked spirit to put me on the right path to do my life's work. I really meant it and of course, spirit answered my prayer.

I was well on my way to becoming a sought-after spiritual teacher. I could demonstrate my knowledge in writing and in speech. I had gained the confidence of many people even though my life was a mess. I was involved in a triangle relationship with a married man. I was up to my neck in debt. My children were unhappy and acting out. I kept teaching and writing. I convinced myself that it was a test and if I kept doing the spiritual work everything would work itself out. It didn't matter that I was miserable as long as I was able to keep up a good front. The facade continued for quite a while, then I prayed and the walls came tumbling down.

One of my students became seriously ill. She was in the hospital. It was my duty as her spiritual teacher to go see her but I was otherwise occupied. My male friend had told me that he was going back to his wife. I had never told anyone that he was still with her. I led everyone to believe things were fine with us. I had no one to talk to. I couldn't admit that I had been lying all along. I retreated to my bed to cry. When my student called, I promised to do something for her. I hung the telephone up and forgot all about it.

When my student was released from the hospital she called me. Refusing to admit my own troubles, I told her I had done what I was supposed to do. That something involved another person. In essence I lied to the other person. When I tried to get in touch with that person, I couldn't. My intent was to backtrack my steps and do what I should have done in the first place. Months passed and everything seemed to calm down. My student got better. My boyfriend came back. Life was livable again.

Every now and then, the student would raise the issue. I always brushed it off and told her I was trying to locate the person. I tried for six months to get in touch with this person, to no avail. She didn't push the issue and neither did I.

One bright Saturday the telephone rang. It was a friend of the person I had trying to reach. He told me he had spoken to my student. She had expressed her concerns. He had contacted the person I had been trying to reach. He had no idea about what my student was saying. Could I please clear this matter up. My ears got hot. My head was swimming. My lie was about to unravel. My student would know I had lied. My friend would know I had not done what I was supposed to do and his friend would know I had lied on him. You get exactly what you pray for. You may not like it, but you will get it.

I told my friend I would clear it up. I didn't know what to do. I had to save face. No, I had to get on the path. I didn't want anyone to know what I had done. They already knew. But I could fix it. I couldn't think. I couldn't speak. I sat down on the bed and cried. Crying is so wonderful. It really purges the poison in our mind. The key is to cry with an agenda. As I cried, I got in touch with everything I felt. I was tired of trying to live up to the false image I had created. I was tired of pleasing people. I was tired of lying, making myself out to be something I was not. I was scared of failing. I was scared of succeeding. I really felt alone in the world. I had been trying to make people like me. I was really confused. I had no idea who I was or what I really wanted to do. I wished everybody would leave me alone so I could take time to get myself together. I was born Sunday. Every truly transforming experience I have had has occurred on a Saturday. I now realize that if I deal with the pain on Saturday, I will be reborn on Sunday.

My first instinct was to lie. I couldn't face the fact that everyone would know what I had done. I had failed in my responsibilities as a spiritual teacher. I had lied. I had misappropriated someone's money. I had been involved in a relationship with a married man. What would people think about me? What would this mean to the following I had built up? How would I ever face these people again? My ego was frantic. It kept telling and showing me images of my destruction. I saw people laughing at me, ignoring me and taunting me. I could hear the stories and see people's reactions. I thought about all the people who would find out and what they would say. I finally admitted that I didn't care. I wanted to get right within myself. It was then I knew the strength of my spirit. I truly wanted to do the right thing, so I did.

I went to my desk and took out a pad. I wrote my student and my friend. I told them exactly what had happened. I admitted to the lie. I explained my motives without blaming anyone else and I asked for forgiveness. By the time I had wrote the two letters, I wasn't crying any more. I felt peaceful and strong. It wasn't as bad as I thought it would be. I felt free. I mailed the letters and locked myself in my bedroom for 16 days. I didn't answer the telephone. I didn't talk to my children or anyone else. I knew a part of me was going to die in that room, but I also knew I was ready.

So many of us think that if we act like a thing doesn't exist, it will go away. When you are on a spiritual path, you must come face to face with yourself and all of who you are. It is only through this process that you will grow and become the embodiment of a true spiritual consciousness. We cannot teach what we do not know. We cannot talk what we do not walk. If we resist this truth, we create pain for ourselves. Learning and growing spiritually does not have to be painful. We make it painful by resisting the unpleasant parts of ourself. This is the purification process. We must clean ourselves out in order to be clean. We must face and release the thoughts, habits and beliefs which limit us. The fears of the old self must die in order for us to be reborn. In order to do this, we must embrace and live by a code of conduct which embraces spiritual law.

In the quest for spiritual purification, enlightenment and evolution, there are specific principles and understandings one must accept and incorporate into a life philosophy. The "Spiritual Code of Conduct" provides a basic framework for the development of individual desire, thought and action which embodies the true nature of spirit. It is not enough to pray, meditate and visualize. One must reprogram their thinking and indoctrination to encompass the principles of universal law. Purification embodies more than the elimination of toxins and meat from the diet. True spirituality requires acceptance of "self" as an expression of the Creator and recognition of that same quality in all others. The Bahi faith teaches, "Nearness to God is likeness to God," which means Godlike principles must govern our behavior at all times. Our actions must be guided by spirit.

The Spiritual Code of Conduct requires accepting your "oneness" with the Creator as the source of power, knowingness, truth and order in your life. The Code is judgment free. It is the "I Am" principle which acknowledges every individual as a unique expression of the

Creator, on a mission to serve the whole. For the African American woman, the following principles comprise a Spiritual Code of Conduct which will result in the purification of the individual for the evolution of the entire group.

Unconditional Love—Not to be confused with lust, or love of one because they love you. Eliminates fear.
To see everyone and everything as an extension of yourself, and to act towards them as you would want to be treated, is a sign of unconditional love; surrender of judgment, criticism and ego is imperative. Evaluated by your ability to see the best possible outcome in any given situation.

Truth—Not to be confused with what you think or know. Truth is consistent and will not harm anyone. Eliminates ego.
A spiritual empowerment requires you to accept truth, speak truth, teach truth and seek truth. Truth is not what you believe based on your individuality. Truth is consistent. It reveals and produces strength and peace for everyone. Evaluated by the question: "Do I accept what is rather than what I think it is?"

Willingness—Not to be confused with willfullness or doing whatever you want.
Willingness is the surrender of self-centered desire. Eliminates limitation of thought and action. To be willing to do whatever is in accordance with spiritual law whether you want to or not. An act of faith. Evaluated by the question: "Is my will greater than God's will?"

Righteousness—Not to be confused with "I want to be right." Eliminates manipulation.
The purification of desires and thought based on truth.

You must do what is right in consideration of all involved. Evaluated by the question: "What is the best possible thing to do/say that will create harmony or balance for all?"

Responsibility—Not to be confused with self-sacrifice and self-denial, or actions that impress others. Eliminates blame.
To be consciously accountable for every desire and thought which manifests itself as an action by you. Evaluated by the questions: "How did I contribute to this situation, circumstance, in which I find myself?" "What have I learned as a result of what I am experiencing?"

Discipline—Not to be confused with selfishness, or self-denial. Eliminates procrastination.
Thoughts and actions to manifest in an orderly and consistent relationship to goals and responsibilities. Evaluated by the question: "Am I doing all I must do to reach my goal without harming myself or others?"

Humility—Not to be confused with being a doormat or sacrificing the self to please someone else. Eliminates feeling used.
Your actions must be prompted from a posture of service to the Creator and not for the satisfaction of the ego. It is giving and doing for the sake of it and not to promote self. Evaluated by the question: "What do I hope to gain for myself?"

Compassion—The ability to place yourself in the position of another without judgment or criticism, treating the other as you would want to be treated.
Evaluated by the question: "Am I my brother's keeper? No. I am my brother."

Perseverence—Not to be confused with stubbornness or

reckless action. Eliminates mental and physical confusion.

Dedication and commitment to a stated goal, even in the face of adversity. When moving in truth and righteousness one must know that the best will manifest. Evaluated by the question: "Am I being true to my stated goal?"

Patience—Not to be confused with laziness or inactivity. Eliminates hasty actions.

Accepting the concept of divine order for the perfect outcome of all situations in relation to the Creator's goals. Evaluated by the question: "Is this the best time for the manifestation of my desire?"

Speaking With A Conscious Tongue—Not to be confused with speaking your mind or saying what you feel. Eliminates negative words and energy.

Because every word we utter is a prayer, we must always speak in a manner that promotes a spiritual principle. We must be mindful that our words do not create negative energy for ourselves or anyone else. Evaluated by the question, "Why am I saying this?"

Selflessness—Not to be confused with doing something to get something, or acting to get acceptance. Eliminates quest for ruthless power.

Commission of certain acts without renumeration aimed at nurturing the young and regeneration of universal truths. Evaluated by the question: "What can I do to help someone else?"

Tithing—Not to be confused with paying someone for spiritual work. Eliminates supporting unworthy spiritual sources.

Requires one to give freely to the source of their spiritual education for the purpose of maintaining that source. The universal law of reciprocity states that what we give, we get back one hundredfold. Tithing enacts this law.

Adherence to the code in the daily interaction with family, social and business relations will create a shift of mental and physical energy. The result will be a more balanced, harmonious and orderly approach to activity. For the African American, the Spiritual Code of Conduct is in keeping with the ancient Egyptian principle of "Maat," symbolized by the feather.

THE CODE OF MAAT

Maat is the intuitive sense of law and order according to divine and universal law, not the law of man. It is learning from within, based on who you are and what you have come to this life to learn and do. It is the foundation of life, symbolizing truth, righteousness and moral conduct (intent). Maat encourages love, the principle of giving and asking nothing in return. It judges the heart, not the deed or external appearances. It is the universal law which evaluates the intent of your criticism and the truth of your actions.

It is believed that when we pass from the physical to the spiritual plane (life to death), Maat is the principle by which our life will be measured. If your heart was placed on a balancing scale with the feather of Maat, would the scale balance out? Using the Spiritual Code of Conduct as the tool by which we measure our lives creates peace within our heart toward others and within the world. It is this peace which will balance the scale of Maat.

On the path toward spiritual enlightenment, it is easy to mistake the lower nature of the ego as a new-found spiritual power. We can justify almost anything by saying,

"spirit told me . . ." or "My spirit says, thinks, feels . . . "
However, if we have not achieved a true spiritual consciousness, we are simply using spirit as a scapegoat for
the ego. One must be cautious not to allow human
emotions to color the principles of spirituality. Remember, spirit is energy. Consequently there are spirits of light
as well as spirits of a lower, darker nature. Spirits of light
follow universal law. Dark spirits satisfy human lusts and
weaknesses. We create energy and attract spirits based on
the level of our consciousness.

As human beings, we are first committed to the
satisfaction of our physical senses. We are led by those
things we can see, hear, touch and taste. We are socialized in a society which emphasizes tangible evidence as
a source of security and control. We are trained and
encouraged to accumulate tangible things to substantiate
what we know and have. A brilliant, enlightened spiritual
being becomes suspect without a degree; yet, a dark-
hearted egoistical individual with a degree is held up as
a model being. As difficult as it may be, those on a spiritual
path must seek to have a clear conscious and personal
sense of integrity, regardless of whether or not the outside
world recognizes the light.

Unfortunately, to satisfy the demands of our physical
nature usually puts us in violation of universal law.
Because our physical senses are enslaved to our will and
ego, we are motivated to be in control of people and
situations. Universal law promotes freedom of choice and
movement. Will and ego, ruled by emotions and perceptions, places the individual self first while spirit recognizes
the Creator as the first cause. The physical nature will use
dark energy to achieve light, while spirit moves in the light

to achieve enlightenment. Unless we adhere to spiritual principles to govern our thoughts, conduct and words, we will create harm and discord. In this environment, dark spirits find their strength and motivation.

What we draw to us is what we are. Whatever the condition of our external life, it is a reflection of our internal state. For every physical sense, there is a spiritual equivalent.

The physical eyes are related to the third or spiritual eye, located in the center of the forehead. The third eye sees truth from a universal perspective; physical eyes can only relate what we know.

The sense of hearing is related to the heart. The heart is centered in unconditional love while our hearing is limited emotions.

The sense of touch is related to the life center located in sexual organs. Touch is a function of desire which must be purified by denial and sacrifice. The sex organs are the root to satisfaction of all lusts, not just sexual.

The sense of smell is related to the solar plexus located in the center (stomach) region of the body. The solar plexus is the seat of our ability to make decisions while the stomach is satisfied by the conscious will.

When we are motivated by satisfaction of the physical without consideration for the spiritual, we fall into the trap of doing what feels good. What feels good is not always best for us in the final outcome. When we experience misfortune, delay and disappointment in our physical life, it is a reflection of an imbalance in one of our spiritual centers.

Women are desperate to find a way out of their suffering, pain and immobility. Most of us want peace and happiness. We are taught to look for happiness in things and people. We are indoctrinated to seek peace in what we are doing rather than in what we are. Most of us are trained to be dependent and irresponsible, holding someone else responsible for our happiness. We live according to roles as opposed to purpose. These are the live issues which take us out of alignment with the laws of the universe. We will remain slaves to our weaknesses, fears and the lower nature of our human consciousness until we surrender our will and ego to spirit. As long as we continue to do what we "think" is right without clear guidelines to know what is right, we will remain limited.

A spiritual brother of mine who is of the Bahai faith teaches that the only way to determine if you are in compliance with the spiritual code of conduct is through a process of self accounting. We must take ourselves into account each day to determine if we are moving in a spiritual light. This brother taught me that before retiring each day you must review your actions from the last thing you did to the first. After listing your activities, you should ask yourself the following questions:

Who did I serve today?
Who did I help today without asking for payment?
Who did I share my knowledge with today?
Did I speak consciously today?
Did I mean what I said today?
Did I keep the agreements I made today with myself?
With others?

As much as possible, your thoughts, behavior and words should be in alignment with the code. When you miss the mark, don't beat yourself. Forgive yourself by making a commitment to do better the next day. With patience, perseverance and a conscious commitment, you will become more consciously enlightened.

SPIRITUAL CODE OF CONDUCT
Oh my Glorious Lord, help me to refrain
    from every irregular inclination;

To subdue every rebellious passion;

To purify the motives of my conduct;

To conform myself to that meekness which no provocation can ruffle;

To that patience which no afflication can overwhelm;

To that integrity which no self interest can shake,
    that I may be qualified to serve Thee and
        teach Thy word

              'Abdu'l Bahá

Chapter 15

Precautions For Your Journey

The level of crisis we create in our lives is amazing. It is so unnecessary—but amazing. For me it was a financial crisis. My life was a series of somebody coming to cut something off, repossess something or to put me out of somewhere. As a child, I was never taught how to budget. Like my parents, I lived hand to mouth. I believed I did not have enough money to save, so I never did. I wanted so much, while believing I had too little. When I did have money, I bought what I wanted in rebellion to my lack of things. When the financial crisis hit me, I would beat myself up for what I had done with my money.

I had a million reasons for not paying my bills. My public assistance budget wasn't adequate; the children needed shoes; I deserved a new dress. Many of my friends who were also on public assistance would sympathize with my plight. We would borrow and lend money among ourselves as we bemoaned our fate. One day, at a round-table discussion of our poverty, one of my friends suggested that "someone must have done something" to me. That was the only explanation for my continued bad luck. She told us that where she had come from people would burn candles, make powder and drop it at your door and do things with your picture. If they wanted your man, they would go to all lengths to make your life miserable. Some of the women at those discussions laughed. Some asked probing questions. I kept my mouth shut and made a mental note.

Without a clear understanding of what to look for, I set out to find a spiritualist. The newspaper was full of advertisements. I was drawn to an ad which read, "It takes a special power to clear financial blocks—I've got it." I called to make an appointment.

As soon as I walked in the door I knew it was a mistake, but I thought I was desperate. The waiting room was cluttered with people, furniture, nicknacks, newspapers and dust. None of that bothered me. It was the darkness. The room felt dark. When Dr. Bones called me, I jumped to my feet. He led me into the kitchen where he had a candle, several glasses of water, an opened Bible and hundreds of jars of stuff. He turned the pages of the Bible and without asking my name, began to tell me about my life. My mother's death. My neglected childhood. How many children I had and the order of their birth. My faltering relationship and my financial devastation.

I was shocked. He made up a little jar of something. I was to wash my hands three times a day for ten days. I gave him $50. If things did not improve, I was to come back in ten days. I was sticking the key in my apartment door before I realized it. Ten days later, the telephone was off, I owed two months rent and the refrigerator was bare. I called. Dr. Bones instructed me to come right over.

This time, Dr. Bones let me in on the seriousness of my problem. Somebody had fixed my boyfriend so that he would leave me. He had brought an evil spirit into my house, that is why our relationship was going sour. The spirit was in my stomach. I had to take my panties off and let him place some "Run Devil Run" oil in my vagina. Reality hit me with a blast. It would cost another $75, with guaranteed results.

"Excuse me, Dr. Bones, but I don't understand the relationship between my vagina and the money in my purse."

He became very stern.

"If you want to get your life together, stop acting foolish. I see hundreds of people a week. What makes you think I want you!"

My memory scanned the waiting room. I was the only person younger than 50.

"I'll tell you what. Give me the oil and I'll put it where it should be."

Reluctantly he handed me the bottle of oil and pointed me to the bathroom. My pants were around my ankles. I was smelling the bottle of oil when the doctor crept into the bathroom. When I looked at him, I instantly knew that my telephone bill would not be paid and that I would probably get evicted. "Please don't" were the only words that I could speak. Scrambling into the corner, trying to pull my pants up, I dropped the bottle of oil.

"Oh shit!" He screamed at me. "Look what you're doing!"

Dr. Bones was on his knees trying to save the oil. I

stepped over him, grabbed my things and left. Three blocks away, I started crying. I cried all the way home.

Why is it that we must be in a state of desperation before we look for God. Maryann Williamson, author of *A Return To Love,* says "A nervous breakdown is an opportunity for a spiritual breakthrough—the chance for God to clean up your spirit and life. A nervous condition means you are not getting the point." I was definitely on the verge of a nervous breakdown.

I spent the afternoon moping around the house. Each time I thought about the "doctor," I started crying. How was I supposed to know he was a ripoff. He was using a Bible. The $125 I gave him would have paid the telephone bill. I sat on the edge of the bed for hours letting the thoughts flood my mind. I saw the newspaper on the floor. Without thinking I picked it up and started thumbing through. A little below the advertisement for Dr. Bones I saw, "Free consultation by telephone." How dumb can I be? Dumb enough to call. I went to the corner telephone booth. The line was busy for 15 minutes. On the first ring, a woman answered by saying, "Let us pray."

For the next several minutes, a soft melodic voice filled my mind. I was told how beautiful I was and how much God loved me. I heard a plea go up for my clarity, safety and peace. I was reminded that anything I needed to know, I already knew. I was told that anything I wanted or needed, I already had. I was instructed to confess my heart, ask for forgiveness and guidance. I was told to get "still" and let the love of the Almighty fill my mind. I was further instructed not to eat or speak for the next 6 hours and that the answer would come. It didn't matter what the question was.

In 14 days, I was to put $25 in an envelope and sent it to Post Office Box GOD, Brooklyn, New York. I went home and followed all instructions. Seven days later the telephone was back on, the refrigerator was full and the rent was paid up to date. I put $100 in an envelope and mailed it to Mother Mary.

*

This is not an easy task you are about to undertake, yet it is a necessary one. You are about to alter your conscious and unconscious state. You are attempting to shift and manipulate energy. You are moving to touch the foundation of your being. You are going to meet challenges and obstacles. You, yourself, are going to be the greatest obstacle you will encounter.

Change is difficult. Change is frightening. Change is constant. Change is inevitable. Change is an inside job. As you begin to change, you are going to resist. You will gravitate to what is known, what is familiar, even those thoughts, habits, and people which have not been positive in your life. Remember, once you commit yourself to a path of spiritual growth, spirit will give you what you need, when you need it. Do not be surprised by anything you see, hear or experience which shakes some belief you have held. Simply affirm for truth to be revealed, and for strength and understanding to be provided.

You may begin to notice that your thoughts and feelings about certain things and people will change. Trust your head. Understand that feelings are "e-motions," the energy that moves us from one place to another. You are moving from one level of spiritual consciousness to another. Your emotions will move you from thinking and behaving in a nonproductive manner to a more productive manner by revealing to you all nonproductive forces. Remember however, the choice to move remains yours. Spirit will not move it for you. Affirm for clarity and direction to act and move in the best way for the benefit of all concerned.

You should not discuss the intimate details of your ritual, experiences and revelations with too many people. If you are not clear or unsure of anything you experience, pray and meditate for guidance. Know that "when the student is ready, a teacher will appear." Do not look for someone to do it for you. What you want is someone or something to provide you with guidance and assistance. This may come in the form of a book, a lecture, a dream, a television commercial or jingle. Be on the lookout for your answer and above all "trust your head," it will tell you what is right for you.

Another helpful hint is to keep a journal of your thoughts and experiences. This is a way to keep your mind clear while you are evolving and to solidify your thoughts. Writing lays before you what is hard to capture in thought. When you can read your thoughts you find the realities, as well as the inconsistencies. Above all, writing is a release. You can release and clear your mind to receive new and improved information, which will aid in your growth.

Finally, be very careful of what you say during your development process. Never say "never." Avoid "I can't," "I am weak," "I am confused." Keep your thoughts and words to and about yourself positive and encouraging. Do not talk about what you do not want, "I don't want to stop," "go," "fail." Speak about what you want in positive terms. Do not condemn, judge or speak negatively about anyone or anything during this time. As your spiritual vision and understanding sharpen, you will recognize that things are not always as they seem. You want to avoid negative pronouncements which you may later be forced to retract. Above all stay up, stay open, stay in tune. Spirit will pave the way. Walk in balance with faith in your divinity.

Chapter 16

Now That I've Got It, What Am I Supposed To Do With It?

You have just taken a journey through "Precautions For Your Journey, Spirituality 101." You have all the basics—breathing, prayer, meditation—and how and when to do it all. The question is now, what are you going to do? How are you going to apply this information and knowledge to produce positive results in your life? Are you going to apply it? Finally, what do you expect as a result?

In order to realize the maximum results from using the information presented here, you must know what you are looking for. Your expectations will determine the outcome of anything you do. Spiritual growth and development is not a quick fix or a way out. It is an inheritance you receive for patient, diligent and conscious searching. There is no way anyone can tell you what to expect or when you will find it. It is a process, much like the turning of the leaves, the growth of your body parts and the greying of hair. It just happens. You cannot pinpoint the exact moment, you just know it will happen. Your spiritual realization and growth are the same way.

Nothing can help you unless you BELIEVE it can help you. If you have read this book believing it will provide you with information, that is exactly what you will get. If you believe the information can help you achieve peace, strength, health or good fortune, you will see it manifest in your life. If you believe you are too far gone, too messed up, too confused to make sense of it, reading this book has been a waste of your time. You and your beliefs are the key factor.

There will be people who are in total disagreement with 75% of what has been shared. There will be others who will use some and discard the rest. To others, this will be the revelation they have prayed to receive. No matter which category you fit in, this book will bring you exactly what you have been looking for. Actually, this book does not tell you anything you do not already know. The keys to your kingdom are within you. Having the keys however can be very frustrating if you do not know which doors they fit. What this book does is to structure the mechanics. Spirit will give you exactly what you need, when you need it, if you are honestly searching. In anticipation of the many questions your mind has conjured up, the following is offered to assist you.

1 - Worshipping or paying homage to ancestors is not replacing God. When we praise and uplift the energy (spirit) of our ancestors we are simply saying, "Thank you for paving the way." It is not primitive or anti-Christ. In fact, Christ is an ancestor. We should and do praise his energy.

2 - It does not matter what your religious affiliation may be—everyone, anyone, can pay homage to their ancestors. Ancestral altars and shrines provide a place for symbolic offerings. However, you can praise them in your heart and mind if you believe they can/do/will hear you.

3 - Breathing is the key to quieting your mind for meditation. The deeper you breathe, the more energy you provide your spiritual self.

4 - When you begin the meditation process it will be difficult to keep still and still your mind. There is nothing wrong with you! Try listening to some soothing instrumental music. (Flute or piano are most soothing). Listen intently to the music. Breathe to the rhythm. When the thoughts come into your mind, simply think, "Peace."

5 - You can forgive, no matter what the person has done to you. As long as you do not forgive, you are locked into the memory of the event. One way to begin is to forgive yourself for anything negative you have ever thought, said, or done against anyone.

6 - When you begin the forgiveness process, you probably will not believe or feel what you are saying. Do it anyway. And yes, you can forgive people after they die.

7 - It does not matter what you have done; whether you consider yourself religious or not, you can pray. The divine energy of the Creator is within you. When you pray, you are in essence praying to yourself—and you already know what you have thought, said, or done. The Creator knows too.

8 - There will be occasions when you feel like you just can't pray or meditate. Take 2 minutes, sit still and do it any way!

9 - Yes, you can teach children to meditate.

10 - Any process shared in this book can be altered to meet your needs. Simply spend a few moments in silence and ask your spirit to guide you.

11- The rewards of spiritual development are a peaceful heart, a clear head and the ability to   take active control of your life.

12 - You can use the Bible, Koran, Bhagavad-Gita   or any holy book you choose to get spiritual   guidance. Take a few deep breaths; place the book in the center of your forehead; think about the situation facing you; using your right hand open the book to any page. Read the first 7 lines on the right hand page. Your solution will be there.

13 - If you pray for something and you do not see   the answer, consider the following:
  - Is what you want good for you?
  - Will you or anyone else be hurt by you having it?
  - Are you ready for the responsibility of having it?
(Doubt, worry and fear uproot the seeds of prayer.)

If you can answer these questions affirmatively and the answer to your prayer has not manifested—the issue is probably patience.

14 -If you want to know if the development process is working ask yourself: 1) How do I feel about it? 2) What do I believe? Remember, what you believe determines what you see.

15 -Always remember, spirit and the Creator do the work. Your job is to see (in your mind) what you want or where you want to be. The work will be done for you and through you.

16 - How you can ensure you will benefit from the development process:
    - *Ask For It*
    - *Give Thanks For It*
    - *Plan For it*
    - *Believe It Is Yours Now!*

"The steps of the good are ordered by the Lord."

You now have your marching orders.

It is up to you to take the first step.

Just do it!